MOSES' ARK

Stories from the Bible

MOSES' ARK

STORIES FROM THE BIBLE

Alice Bach & J. Cheryl Exum

Illustrated by Leo and Diane Dillon

Delacorte
Press

Acknowledgments

We are grateful to Professors Yairah Amit of Tel Aviv University, David J. A. Clines of the University of Sheffield, and Philip J. King of Boston College for their careful readings of our stories and their helpful suggestions. Because they know their right hand from their left, they were able to keep our ark afloat, fill the pharaoh's cup with mango juice, and offer two pressings of the finest olive oil.

Published by
Delacorte Press
Bantam Doubleday Dell Publishing Group, Inc.
666 Fifth Avenue
New York, New York 10103

Text copyright © 1989 by
Alice Hendricks Bach and J. Cheryl Exum
Illustrations copyright © 1989 by
Leo and Diane Dillon

Library of Congress Cataloging in Publication Data

Bach, Alice.
Moses' ark : stories from the Bible
retold by Alice Bach and J. Cheryl Exum
illustrated by Leo and Diane Dillon.
p.   cm.
ISBN 0-385-29778-5
1. Bible stories, English—O.T.   I. Exum, J. Cheryl.
II. Dillon, Leo.   III. Dillon, Diane.   IV. Title.
BS551.2.B24   1989
222'.09505—dc19   89-1069
CIP
OG

Manufactured in the United States of America
September 1989
Designed by Jane Byers Bierhorst
10 9 8 7 6 5 4 3 2 1

for Rebecca Cockrell Exum,
who taught the pleasures of a good story,
and for Lou and Dorothy Martyn,
who know the stories behind the stories

CONTENTS

Introduction

This collection retells stories from the Bible, ranging from Genesis through Kings. Because the ancient Hebrews told stories in a very different way from modern storytellers, it is not enough to translate their tales into our language. We have tried to capture the spirit of the original stories and to bring out nuances and emphasize details that many translations simplify or miss altogether.

Biblical tradition stresses the importance of the twelve tribes of Israel, whose ancestors are the twelve sons of the patriarch Jacob. Besides twelve sons, Jacob also had one daughter, Dinah. The thirteen stories in this volume are symbolic of the thirteen children of Jacob. Our selection was made with a view toward illustrating the Bible's diversity. Along with the more familiar tales of the garden, the flood, and the exodus plagues, we have included lesser-known stories, such as Saul's encounter with the medium at Endor, Jotham's fable, and some of David's less admirable adventures. We have included a number of stories that portray women as strong figures, among them the defiant women

who save the chosen people by saving the infant Moses, the prophet and judge who led the Israelite army to defeat the Canaanites at the river Kishon, and the wise ruler of the land of Sheba.

As far as we know, *Moses' Ark* is the only collection of Bible stories based on the original language, informed by the fruits of contemporary biblical scholarship, and written especially for children. Working from the original Hebrew text, we have highlighted features of the stories available only to readers of the original. A prime example is found in the story of Moses' birth. We are all familiar with Noah's ark, but the reader of the Hebrew text knows that Moses, too, has an ark. The Hebrew word *tevah* used for Noah's ark appears in only one other place in the Bible, referring to the "basket" Moses' mother makes before setting him afloat on the Nile. The allusion, lost in most translations, is extremely important: both "arks" are vehicles of salvation.

In the same story, the reader of Hebrew recognizes that the Egyptian pharaoh, not one of the Israelites, is the first person to speak of the event that was to become known as the exodus. He is worried that his Hebrew slaves will "go up from the land," the phrase that is found throughout the Bible to refer to the Israelites' exodus from Egypt.

Many puns are available to the reader of Hebrew. Hebrew *'adam*, an "earthling" taken from the ground, *'adamah*, becomes the first human being. Samson's name recalls the Hebrew word for sun, and Delilah's is a pun on night. Solomon's name is related to the word *shalom*, meaning peace or contentment, an idea that also appears in the name Jerusalem. In the notes that appear at the end of each story we have pointed out the puns and word plays we think particularly interesting.

There is much humor in these old stories; the ancients

knew how to prod a proud prophet like Elijah wishing for God to appear to him in the same spectacular fire and smoke that Moses saw. And they could take great delight in Samson's mischievous pranks at the expense of their hated neighbors, the Philistines. Poking fun at enemies is commonplace in the Bible. The ancient authors certainly were casting a cold eye at the Egyptian pharaoh whose "wise solutions" to the problem of Hebrew overpopulation are patently ridiculous. We have sought to capture his foolish character in our retelling.

Retelling involves the filling of gaps. We all fill gaps by supplying our own selection of details when we read stories. For example, the biblical storyteller tells us nothing about life aboard Noah's ark during those drenching forty days and nights. Because today's readers may be curious about different things from ancient listeners, we have filled in the sort of details we think will help the stories come alive for our readers. Some details we can add without scholarly support. Surely all those animals made quite a racket as the rain fell endlessly!

Sometimes we have depended on scholarly findings to tell us what we need to know. Archaeology has provided actual examples to show how people lived and worked: we have remains of houses, city defenses, and water systems, as well as cooking utensils, pottery, tools, and weapons. Scholars have written in great detail about the clear parallels to Moses in the portrayal of Elijah, or the fact that, in the garden story, the gender of the first human being is not specified. Some scholars think the tower of Babel was patterned on the Babylonian ziggurat, a pyramid-shaped temple tower. Since looking at maps is frequently helpful for understanding the action, you might want to consult an atlas listed among the works in our bibliography.

When we began to retell the stories, we wondered about details that the text didn't provide. Oddly enough they were details we hadn't missed in many years of reading the stories. One example occurred in the story about King Solomon. The Bible does not go into detail in describing the gifts the queen of Sheba brought to King Solomon. The Hebrew text says simply, "She came to Jerusalem with a very large retinue, with camels bearing spices, and very much gold, and precious stones." In order to underscore the opulence of the queen, and to give the modern reader an idea of what the royal riches were in the time of Solomon and the queen of Sheba, we have detailed her gifts of spices (not usually valued by today's royalty), and her jewelry, which would still be greatly prized.

All of the items we name were known in biblical times and are either mentioned somewhere in the Bible or known to us from archaeological excavation. Our description of the queen's palanquin, with its sixty servants, is based on the description of Solomon's litter in the Song of Songs. Details about Solomon's feast are drawn from Ahasuerus' feast in the Book of Esther. The riddles and wise sayings with which the queen of Sheba and Solomon entertain each other come from Proverbs, Ecclesiastes, and other biblical books. Since tradition says that Solomon was the author of the Song of Songs, the collection of Proverbs, and the poetry of Ecclesiastes, we have seasoned his story with the flavor of these other biblical books.

Biblical writers were very interested in some sorts of details and not in others. They were amazingly accurate about place names and provided many details about battles. Yet, in the story of Moses' birth, we are not told the names of Moses' mother and father. And listen to this biblical description of the Israelites' dependence on the Philistines'

superior toolmaking skills: "There was no smith to be found throughout the land of Israel . . . so all the Israelites went down to the Philistines to sharpen their plowshares, their mattocks, their axes, and their sickles, and the charge was a pim [two thirds of a shekel] for the plowshares and for the mattocks, and a third of a shekel for sharpening the axes and setting the goads." That's more detail than we might have wished for!

Sadly for those of us who like to know what people look like, the Bible is particularly reticent about personal appearance. Did Moses really have a long flowing beard like the Moses in the movies? Was Elijah short and fat? We are told that Saul was tall; but was he handsome? Was Rahab, the woman who hid the Israelite spies, very beautiful? Was she old or young? What kind of finery did a king like Solomon wear? In keeping with biblical tradition, we have not made up descriptions of our characters' appearances when the Bible has not provided them.

The Bible is also content to tell a piece of an incident. For instance, in the story of Samson, the biblical account says that the Philistines threatened Samson's wife in order to learn the answer to Samson's riddle. But it doesn't expand or fill out that scene. What was she doing when her countrymen approached her? The wedding guests were "feasting" at the wedding but on what sorts of food? At what time of year was the marriage to take place? Did they have music at the wedding? The Bible was not interested in these details, but supplying some of them has made our stories more like modern stories.

As we have said, our filling of these sorts of gaps is based on scholarly research. If you find details in our stories that are not mentioned in another version of that biblical tale, you will know that the clothes, food, or descriptions of places accurately describe that time and region of the world.

There are explanatory notes at the end of each story. They comment on important or unusual aspects of the story and provide insights designed to help the reader understand a little more about the background of the story. We hope after reading our retellings, and the notes about the stories, you will appreciate how many different kinds of stories are to be found in the Bible, how many moments of tenderness and of violence, of bravery and of fear, of joy and of sadness. If you have questions that we have not answered, try looking in some of the books listed in our bibliography. And remember that in the many hundreds of years since these stories were first told, people have not settled on a single interpretation for them. One of the extraordinary things about the Bible is that its readers are still discovering new things in the stories. You may too.

THE

GARDEN OF EDEN

Long ago, before time, the earth was a barren wasteland. Before there were any living things upon the earth, before trees had sprung up or flowers had bloomed, nothing stirred upon the earth. The Lord God had not yet caused it to rain, and there was no human to cultivate the earth. But there was a stream that rose up from the earth to water the face of the ground.

Then the Lord God shaped fine particles of dust into human form and breathed into its nostrils the breath of life. And it became a living being.

God looked around and saw no pleasant place for the human to live. So God planted a garden in Eden and amid the sweet green grasses God put the newly created human being. God walked around the garden considering what else might be made so that the garden in Eden would be beautiful to look at and would provide delicious fruits of all kinds for the

human to enjoy. God set to work making trees. Lemon trees, grapefruit and orange, apple and fig, and pomegranate. Then God caused them to grow and bear ripe fruit. God added every kind of blossoming plant and thick carpets of cool green vegetation to cover the ground. In the middle of the garden God placed the Tree of Life and the Tree of Knowledge.

A river ran through Eden and watered the garden, and from there it divided into four rivers. The first river flowed around the mysterious land of Havilah, where the purest gold and most priceless gems in all the world are found. The second river flowed through the sun parched sands of Ethiopia. The third and fourth rivers framed the desert lands.

The human whom God had made walked around the garden, looking at all the delights God had placed there. Then the Lord God said, "You may enjoy all the fruit from these trees—limes, persimmons, and pears, those purple fruits and the yellow ones too. But you may not eat the fruit of the knowledge tree." The human being nodded. "Remember there is a punishment for eating its fruit. The punishment is death."

God stood back and watched the human being in its new home. The human picked some ripe fruit and ate it. It touched the pale petals of flowers and the rough bark of a tree. Then it sat in the shade of a broad-leafed tree, looking at its own fingers.

"It is not good that the human is alone," God

thought. "I shall make a companion to share this luscious garden, a companion that is just right for it."

Then the Lord God knelt on the ground and began to knead the earth, forming shapes with quick, steady fingers. Legs were pulled from a barrel-shaped belly. God smiled and added a long rope of a nose, ears like palm leaves, and a tail no bigger than a finger. When it was finished, God showed the creature to the human being, who named it Elephant.

Then God gathered up a fresh handful and fashioned a rough-hided creature with stumpy legs and sharp pointed snout. And the human being called it Rhinoceros. God tried a bird with long spindly legs and knotted feet. "Ostrich," said the human being. God continued forming bits of earth into living creatures until all the beasts of the field and the birds of the air had been named.

Then God looked at all the creatures resting in the cool shade; God watched the birds nesting along the curved limbs of the trees, and God decided that none of the creatures who had been made that day was the right companion for the human being.

So God caused a deep sleep to fall upon the human being. While it slept, God took one of its sides, and with the artistry of a sculptor, built another human being. God mended the wound of the first human being and called the creature Man. When the man woke up, he exclaimed with delight, "This is the right companion for me. Bone of my bone and flesh of my flesh, she shall be called Woman because she was

taken out of Man." The woman and the man were naked in their garden, but they were not embarrassed to have God see them.

Of all the wild creatures the Lord God had made, the wisest was the serpent. It was strolling through the garden one day, when it saw the woman and the man gathering fruit near the middle of the garden. Coiling itself along the low-hanging branch of the knowledge tree, it began musing out loud, hoping to attract the woman's attention. "Imagine, the Lord God telling you not to eat any of the delicious fruit that grows in this garden." The serpent caressed a piece of fruit with the tip of its tail.

The woman hurried over to the tree where the serpent had draped itself. "We may eat the fruit of all the trees in the garden except this one," she said. "This one we may not even touch, or we will die." With her toe she absentmindedly wiped the serpent's fragile footprints from the dirt.

"Nonsense," replied the serpent. "You won't die. God is afraid that if you eat this fruit, you will have knowledge you did not have before. You will see good and evil. You will be just like gods."

The woman and the man looked up at the tree. Great clusters of fruit hung just above their heads. Standing under the tree for the first time, the woman appreciated its beauty. Its spicy fragrance delighted her. Surely fruit that looked so appealing and smelled so sweet would be good to eat. The woman wondered

about all the serpent had said, while the man looked at the fruit without curiosity. When she considered that the tree also offered wisdom and knowledge, she took some of its fruit and ate it. She handed a piece to the man and he ate it.

The serpent had been right; they did not die. But in their newfound knowledge they felt embarrassed because they were naked. Quickly they took some of the broad leaves of a nearby fig tree to cover themselves.

In the evening, when the cool breezes began to stir the trees, the couple heard the sound of the Lord God walking around in the garden.

The man grabbed the woman's hand. "Let's hide before God sees us."

God called to the man. "Where are you?"

The woman looked up at the tree as if it might answer for them.

God called to the man a second time. "Where are you?"

"I heard you walking around in the garden and I was embarrassed because I was naked. So I hid myself," the man replied haltingly.

"Who told you that you were naked? Did you eat from the forbidden tree?"

"The woman you created to be my companion— she gave me the fruit and I ate it." The man hid his face from the Lord God.

Then God turned to the woman and said, "What have you done?"

"The serpent tempted me and I ate the fruit from the knowledge tree."

God cast an angry gaze upon the serpent who stood nearby, drawing tiny circles in the dust with one of its feet. "Of all tame animals and all wild animals you alone are cursed! You shall crawl upon your belly and eat the dust of the ground all the days of your life. For all of time, you serpents will be enemies of human beings. They will tread on your heads and you will bite their heels."

To the woman God said, "From the first light of day until the sun has set, you will labor. During rain and drought, seedtime and harvest, your labor will be hard in the fields and in childbirth. Your husband spent no time near my knowledge tree, but you were attracted by it. You desired to be godlike. Now you shall follow and he shall take the lead."

To the man God said, "Because you followed your wife and ate from the knowledge tree, the ground shall be cursed from this day forth. No longer will the earth yield its abundance to you, but rather thorns and thistles. By the sweat of your brow you will earn your living from the soil all the days of your life. For from the dust you were taken and to dust you shall return."

The Lord God made the man and his wife clothes from skins to take the place of the leaves they had used to cover themselves. But God worried that humans were becoming too much like gods, now that they had come to know good and evil. "If they live

here, enjoying the freedom of the garden, they might eat from the Tree of Life. They must be stopped. Only God can live forever!"

So the Lord God sent them from Eden to work the ground from which God made the human being. As they left the garden the woman and her husband looked back one final time at the green and gentle place that had been their home. At the entrance they saw that the Lord God had stationed cherubim and a quivering sword of flame, so they could not approach the Tree of Life.

Notes

This story is one of two creation stories found in the opening chapters of the Book of Genesis. The first, which begins with the first verse of Genesis and ends with the first half of the fourth verse in chapter 2, presents humanity as the climax of a series of acts of creation. Male and female are created simultaneously in the image of God, and there is no indication that only one couple is meant. In our story, which begins where the first account leaves off and continues through chapter 3, a human being is created, then a garden, then trees, animals, and finally a second human being. It is not entirely clear whether the first human created is a man or simply a human being in the generic sense. The Hebrew word *'adam*, from which we get the proper name Adam, can refer to a man, but most often it is used as a collective term for humanity. We have chosen not to specify the sex of the first human until the point in the story

where we have two human beings, clearly a man and a woman.

What did this first human being look like? We don't know, just as we do not know what kind of fruit (it was not an apple!) grew on the Tree of Knowledge—these unexplained things belong to a time before time. From the "side" of the first human being a woman is formed. The word is traditionally translated "rib" because the rabbis said it meant "rib," but nowhere else in the Bible does it have this meaning. We take the term to be intentionally ambiguous, and have given it the more likely meaning "side." A possible interpretation of the text's meaning is that when the side of the human is taken away to form the woman, what remains after the divine surgery is a man.

In the account of the eating of the forbidden fruit, the woman considers the possibilities offered by the Tree of Knowledge and is motivated by the desire to acquire godlike powers; the man is silent throughout her theological discussion with the serpent and simply eats. The text insists that both her active and his passive disobedience require punishment. In bitterly ironic "poetic justice," the active offender is made subordinate to the passive one.

The story does not function as a justification for the subordination of woman to man (a situation that needed no justification in the ancient world). Rather it describes life's universal hardships as women and men experienced them, sweating out a living from the uncooperative Palestinian soil. In addition women were given the extra burden of bearing many children. Men lived to about the age of forty. Women had a shorter life span because of the risks associated with childbearing.

THE FLOOD

When the earth was still young and people had not yet been scattered among distant lands, life was difficult. People had to work hard to raise enough food from the ground that God had cursed because Adam and Eve had eaten the fruit of the knowledge tree against God's will. As time passed, the many descendants of Adam and Eve grew more and more wicked. In their hearts lodged dark thoughts and meanness. Brothers and sisters fought with each other and wished each other harm. People did not treat one another with respect and kindness. Cruelty and violence swelled all over the earth. When the Lord God saw how corrupt everything had become, God vowed to destroy all that had been created on earth.

"I shall blot out human beings, whom I made from the dust of the ground. I shall destroy every person and every animal, even the insects that creep on the

ground and the birds that fly among the clouds. For I am sorry I created them."

Among the descendants of Eve and Adam only one was righteous and just and God was glad God had made him. His name was Noah.

When Noah was born, his father Lamech declared that one day his son would be special. "From the hard work of our lives, sweating each day to grow food from the hard ground, this son of mine will bring us rest."

After God had determined to destroy all that had been created, God told Noah of his plan. "I'm going to get rid of them all, vile creatures who have filled the earth with their violence. But I shall spare you, Noah. You and your family have pleased me. This is what you must do to survive the time that is approaching.

"Make yourself an ark from gopher wood. There should be rooms inside the ark; it should be covered on the outside with pitch to make sure that it is waterproof. You must make a roof for the ark and a door on one side; the ark should have three decks. The roof should hang over the top deck to protect it from the strong winds and rain. The bottom deck should have high sturdy sides to protect it from the swells of powerfully curling waves. The ark must be very large and it must be seaworthy."

As God talked, Noah listened quietly and said nothing.

"I have decided to bring a great flood upon the earth. Waters shall rain down from heaven upon the land until there is no more land to be seen. Every

creature shall perish in the flood except you and your family. I am sorry in my heart that I ever made this earth. Nothing that lives on the earth shall remain."

Noah remained silent while God continued.

"I shall establish my covenant with you and you shall come into the ark, where you shall be safe, you and your wife and your sons and their wives. Also you shall bring into the ark two of every kind of animal. A female and male of each beast from the field and bird from the air, cattle and creeping things too. All these creatures you shall keep alive in the ark, during the time of the howling winds and swirling waters. It is my plan that the ark will protect you and the animals while the rains cleanse the land. You shall be safe while the evil of the earth is swallowed up in the waters I shall send down from the heavens."

The sky began to darken; it was almost nightfall. Still Noah had not spoken a word.

"Be sure to take every sort of food with you and store it carefully. Grains for the animals, lettuces and lentils, fruits and berries. All the food that I caused to grow on the earth to keep you alive."

Remembering all that God had said, Noah went home and began to gather gopher wood.

Noah and his wife worked from sunup until it was too dark to see the nails that held the boards of the ark together. She hammered and he sawed the beams. She measured and marked the long boards; he stirred the vats of pitch. Their sons, Shem, Ham, and Japheth, smeared the pitch all over the outside of the ark, along its slanted roof, across the three decks, around

the deep-bellied hold of the boat. For days they worked as a family, hurrying to carry out the detailed orders of the Lord God.

Shem, Ham, and Japheth gathered grain and poured it into large storage jars in one of the rooms of the ark. Their wives found fruit and tender leaves and shoots for the animals to eat. In obedience to God's orders, they stored melons and figs and ripe pears. They cut rhubarb and squash and brought in baskets of cucumbers and potatoes. When Noah realized his sons had left out of the storeroom turnips and sprouts and kohlrabi, vegetables they never liked to eat, he sent them back to the fields. For God had said food of every kind, and Noah intended to follow every direction God had given him.

Noah's wife herded the sheep and goats into one of the rooms, while her husband arranged smaller animals in a nearby pen. Birds nested on the rafters of each room, their chirping echoing through the huge ark.

Outside, the sky was almost dark as night, although it was morning. Rain began to fall. "It's time to go into the ark," Noah thought. When a place had been found for every animal and bird, and their sons and their sons' wives were safely aboard, Noah and his wife looked out at the land one last time. Then God closed the door firmly, shutting them all inside the sturdy ark.

God opened all the windows of heaven and the rain poured down upon the earth. The rain was falling so heavily that Noah's family could hardly distinguish

between the hillsides and the fields. A few hours later when they went to the window again, the fields and the hillsides had disappeared. Water engulfed the trees and the meadows and the towns—water lay over everything like a dark blanket. And more rain was falling.

Days passed and the rain continued. Inside the ark the animals grew restless. Sometimes the bleating and screeching grew so loud that Noah thought his ears would burst from the noise. Once in a while a fight broke out among the animals, and one of Noah's sons rushed to soothe the frightened creatures.

Days turned into weeks, and the rain continued. The earth seemed as flat and bare as the horizon. Nothing but water and sky could be seen from the window of the ark. Not even the peaks of the craggiest mountains of rock, once so proud against the sky, remained. While the ark tossed and pitched in the waves, time seemed to stand still. God had told Noah the rain would fall for forty days and forty nights. Rain had never before fallen for forty days and forty nights. Neither Noah nor his wife nor their sons nor the wives of their sons could imagine how much rain the Lord God intended to let fall.

The sky was swollen with rain clouds and so dark that Noah and his family could barely tell when day gave way to night. The rooster crowed at all hours. The dogs barked; the lions roared. The jackals howled. No one got much sleep aboard the ark.

The rain had fallen for so long that the tallest mountain peaks were buried under more than fifteen

feet of water. The ark, which looked so large and airy when Noah and his family had settled the animals in each room, was now overcrowded. Restless bears reared up and beat against the walls of the ark. Monkeys hung down dispirited from the rafters. The leopard clawed at the floor. The wives of Noah's sons sang to the animals, but their melody could barely be heard above the caw of the parrot and the pounding of rain upon the roof.

Finally God caused a wind to blow across the earth, and the rains stopped. God closed the windows of heaven so that the rain ceased to fall.

A long time passed before the waters receded enough for the tallest mountain peaks to become visible. Finally the ark came to rest upon the mountains of Ararat.

Noah opened the window of the ark and released a raven, which flew over the waters still covering the land. When the bird did not return, Noah's wife coaxed one of the doves down from the rafters of the ark. Noah then released the dove from the ark, but it could find no place to alight. At dusk it returned to the ark. It lit on Noah's arm and he brought it back inside the ark.

During the first week, the animals came out onto the broad dry decks of the ark. The sun warmed their fur. Fresh breezes blew through the ark, and all the creatures were able to rest. Ham, Shem, and Japheth swept the rooms of the ark; their wives fed the animals on deck. Noah's wife smiled at her husband and he returned the smile.

When Noah thought the waters might have subsided, early in the morning he sent the dove out again to see if there was any dry land. All day he waited on the top deck, hoping the bird would return. As the sun was slipping down behind the mountain peaks, the shadow of the dove fluttered across the water. Noah's wife ran up on deck. The dove flew onto the railing, an olive leaf in its mouth.

Ever so slowly the waters dried up. Trees could be seen on the mountainside; hillsides appeared. One day Noah let the dove fly from the ark, and it did not return that night or the next. So Noah knew the ground must be dry.

In the early morning Noah went down to the lowest deck and scanned the cloudless sky. Almost a year had passed since they entered the ark. Now, at last, the ground was dry!

Once again God spoke to Noah. "Go forth from the ark, you and your wife and your sons and your sons' wives. Bring out all the animals onto the dry land so that they may roam freely and multiply and fill the earth."

The animals began to gather on the decks and left the ark two by two, as they had come in. Gazelle and wild boar; tortoise creeping after ox; ibex and hippopotamus and camel. All the animals were finally able to step onto dry ground.

Noah and his family left the ark that had been their home for the past year. They rejoiced at being able to walk in the fields and dig their toes in the damp earth once again. The fragrance of wildflowers

filled the air. From heaven God called to Noah and his family.

"The earth is yours to enjoy. Be fruitful and multiply. I shall establish my covenant with you and with your children and with their children after them and with all living things on the earth. I promise that never again shall there be a flood to destroy the whole earth. As a sign of my promise I set my rainbow high in the clouds. This symbol will remind future generations of the wickedness that caused the rains to fall and my promise that such a great flood will never happen again.

"Whenever you see the bow, remember my promise to you and to all living creatures never to destroy all life on earth.

"For as long as the earth remains,
Seedtime and harvest, cold and heat,
Summer and winter, day and night,
Shall not cease."

In the distance a donkey brayed. The sheep began grazing on the hillside. The crickets settled into the tall grasses. Noah and his family looked up at the clouds and saw God's rainbow, radiant above them.

Notes

According to Hebrew cosmology, the waters of the deep are held back and prevented from destroying the earth by the

firmament of heaven, a dome above the earth. When God opens windows in the firmament, rain falls upon the earth. When God closes the windows, the rain stops. In the story of the flood, all the windows of heaven are opened, and the chaotic waters of the deep threaten to destroy God's creation. Noah and his family are spared, however, and at the end of the story, God promises never again to destroy the earth by unleashing the watery deep.

The name "Noah" means "rest" in Hebrew. The story connects the name to the expectation, expressed by Noah's father, that Noah would relieve the hard lot that had befallen humanity through Adam and Eve's disobedience.

Throughout the entire biblical story, Noah responds to God's commands in silent obedience. Similarly in our retelling, Noah says nothing.

The idea of a flood destroying the earth is widespread in world literature. In such stories, the human hero chosen to be saved from the deluge takes his wife, family, animals, and birds with him into an ark or ship, constructed according to divine instructions. In the Babylonian Atrahasis Epic, the gods send a flood because people on the earth are so noisy that the gods cannot rest. In the Gilgamesh Epic, the ark-builder Utnapishtim and his wife are granted eternal life after the flood; Noah and his wife, in contrast, die, as is the fate of humanity since the punishment of Adam and Eve.

THE TOWER

There was once a time when all the people on earth spoke the same language. Together they journeyed from the East to the land of Babylon. A wide flat grassy plain stretched out all around them. It was the perfect place to settle, they agreed in one voice.

The people began to make bricks. "Come," they said, "let's make bricks, enough bricks to build ourselves a tower."

Once they had the bricks, they fired them until they were hard. With asphalt for mortar, they began laying bricks to build a city.

"Come," they said, "let's not stop building our tower until its top reaches all the way to heaven!" The wonder of all they could accomplish together made them long for the day when their tower would be completed. "Let's build a city more fabulous than Ugarit and Ebla, more beautiful than Nuzi and Sumer.

"We shall be famous for generations to come! Never has such a splendid structure been built." And they kept making bricks, and firing the bricks until they were hard as stone. Row upon row their tower rose into the sky.

The people's voice rose with their building. "With such a wonderful city we will never have to worry about being scattered throughout different lands. With a tower that reaches to heaven we can be like gods!"

The tower rose higher than the highest trees. Those who had to climb to the top each morning got up earlier than the rest. The massive structure gleamed in the bright sunlight. It resembled a wide pyramid that gradually narrowed as though its top were being pulled up toward heaven. The remarkable tower could be seen from many miles away. Travelers who passed it stopped to admire it. Many were mesmerized by its height and stayed to join the project.

"More bricks here on the top," yelled a worker to his companion.

"Be careful; one side of the tower is three layers higher than the other," an adviser warned several workers. All the people could talk to one another of their dreams for the future, because they spoke the same language.

Working day after day, placing brick upon brick, they watched their tower grow. From the ground the top of the tower was shrouded by clouds. "We will surely reach the heavens," they exclaimed one to another. "There has never been a tower as magnificent as ours. And when we have finished building the

city that surrounds the tower, we shall never be scattered."

God was not pleased.

Day after day the people's growing dream of glory reached as one strong clear sound up to the heavens, like the tower itself. God decided to go down to the earth to take a closer look at the great tower and the city that was beginning to spread across the plains of Babylon.

God was not pleased with the massive structures the people were building by themselves. "All the people on earth speak the same language; they are united in all their efforts. If they're not stopped at once, there's nothing they won't be able to do!"

God resolved to confuse the human language, so that the people would not be able to understand one another. "I shall scatter their town and I shall scatter them as well," God decided.

"Another row of bricks and we'll be able to begin the top section," a proud worker called out to his neighbor.

"Why are you cackling like a chicken?" the man replied with surprise.

"Watch out! Falling bricks!" someone screamed. But her words were merely jangling sounds to those around her.

"What's all the commotion? What do you think you're doing up there? Be careful!" a man hollered, his hands on his hips. Not even his children understood what he had said.

Everyone was speaking in a different language; no

one could understand anyone else. People shouted at each other. When it became clear that speaking loudly or softly, rapidly or slowly, would not help, they fell silent.

There were no more shared jokes, no swapping of gossip. Before long, friendly handshakes became fists. People turned their backs on their neighbors.

And so the tower was left unfinished. What the people had feared most had happened. They were scattered far and wide and forced to settle in many different lands. The city they had begun to build lay in ruins. It was given the name Babylon because God had caused the people there to speak so many different languages that each one seemed to the others to babble.

Never again would the people of the world work together to build a single city.

Notes

The story explains the origin of different languages and the dispersion of humanity among different lands. It takes a humorous look at Babylonian culture, with its magnificent walled cities and imposing towers. The tower itself invites comparison with the Babylonian ziggurats, temples designed to link heaven and earth. The story relates the name Babylon to a Hebrew word meaning "to babble." Surprisingly the pun works in English too.

In the story of the garden, Eve and Adam became "godlike" in their acquisition of knowledge, but God prevented them

from attaining another divine attribute, eternal life, by casting them out of the garden to keep them from the Tree of Life. Unlike Utnapishtim and his wife in the Babylonian flood story, Noah and his wife are not granted eternal life. Here again, human beings attempt to overstep the boundaries set by God. Humanity's desire to scale the heavens is viewed as an attempt to claim divine prerogatives. There is great irony in the juxtaposition of human and divine viewpoints. From the human perspective the tower reaches to the heavens, whereas from God's point of view one must "go down" to take a look at it.

MOSES' ARK

When the Hebrews had been in bondage in Egypt for a long time, a new pharaoh came to power. Day after day he would stand in front of the window in his council chamber, watching his Hebrew slaves at their labor in the fields surrounding the palace. "They are growing more numerous," he complained to his advisers. "There are three men bending over each wheelbarrow."

"They are not like other people. The more work we give them, the harder these Hebrews work," one of his advisers said.

"The more slaves we have, the more fine bricks they can make," said another.

"Remember, they carry our heaviest stones; during the past year they have been the best workers on our pyramids in Lower Egypt."

"We plan to set them to building new storehouses

in the delta, one at Pithom and one at Ramses," a third adviser told him.

Pharaoh turned from the window and began to pace the room. "They are more numerous and mightier than we are." He flung his arms wide, almost overturning a gold statue of Isis inlaid with lapis lazuli. "They might leave! We must make sure they do not make an exodus."

"What is an exodus?" the youngest adviser asked timidly.

Advisers to the pharaoh are expected to know everything. An adviser who asks too many questions is no longer an adviser.

Pharaoh was in a good mood and was pleased to answer the question. "An exodus happens when a whole people together with their cattle and flocks and all their belongings leave the land."

"Such a disastrous thing must not happen here!" they exclaimed as a group. "It would make us look foolish. Who would build our pyramids, fill our storehouses, and harvest our wheat and barley?"

Pharaoh smoothed his embroidered robe of fine white linen and called for some wine and figs to be brought to him. "An exodus will never happen so long as I am pharaoh," he assured them. "I shall make an official decree. I shall put the Hebrews to hard labor."

The advisers exchanged puzzled glances. "That is why you are pharaoh," they said, bowing low and hurrying from the chamber to announce the new decree.

Time passed slowly in the fields and on the building sites of Egypt. The Egyptian overseers stayed close to their Hebrew slaves, making them work harder than ever, as the pharaoh had commanded. The Hebrews were forced to carry heavier loads longer distances. The scalding sun beat down on their backs. The skin on their hands became tough as hide. They were not permitted to return to their quarters until long after the sun had set. But still they bent to their work and to their overseers said nothing.

Pharaoh spent most of the day in his council chamber looking out the window. "What foolish advisers I have gathered around me. Your plan is not working," he shouted to the men gathered in a corner of the room. "Look! Now there are five men bending over each wheelbarrow. I can plainly see that the Hebrews are growing more numerous and mightier. What if they forge their chains into weapons and join our enemies against us?"

The advisers were also worried about the growing vigor of the Hebrews. "In the fields and on the building sites the Hebrews are growing more numerous," they said to one another. "We devise work to break their spirits and still they seem to prosper."

"What if they grow strong enough to try to leave my kingdom?" Pharaoh drained his glass of mango juice and demanded another. "I have devised a plan that will sap the strength of these people. Have the midwives brought to my council chamber. Before the sun has set on this day, I shall have reduced the number of Hebrews."

The advisers exchanged puzzled glances. "That is why you are pharaoh," they said, bowing low and hurrying from the chamber to call the midwives.

Shiphrah and Puah, the midwives, were in their homes eating their midday meal when they received word of the pharaoh's summons. Each woman set out immediately for the palace. Shiphrah arrived first and waited near the gate. A few minutes later she saw Puah, her long robe tucked into her sash, running across the herb garden outside the palace walls. Inside, the Egyptian courtiers were resting. Together the midwives hurried through the quiet palace corridors. Outside in the fields the Hebrews toiled under the sweated glare of the hottest sun of the day.

"What could he want from us?" Shiphrah wondered.

"I have never been called before Pharaoh," said Puah, her face creased with worry.

"We are God-fearing women. We have done no wrong," her companion reminded her.

"But often with Pharaoh wrong is right and right is wrong."

They paused outside the door and waited to be summoned into the presence of the ruler.

"You may rise," Pharaoh said to the prostrate women. He selected a slice of pale green melon from a gold plate and turned his attention to the midwives standing in front of him.

"I have a plan that you are to put into action at once," he told the midwives. "When you assist a Hebrew woman in labor, if she gives birth to a son,

you must kill him, but if it is a daughter, she may live." He ate another slice of melon.

The midwives exchanged nervous glances. "That is why you are pharaoh," they said, bowing low and hurrying from the council chamber.

"Kill babies?" sobbed Puah as they left the palace. "What kind of women does Pharaoh think we are? How can we obey Pharaoh?" She turned to Shiphrah with a fresh spate of tears. "If we don't obey him, we'll bring down his anger upon us."

"Dry your tears." Shiphrah put her arm around Puah's shaking shoulders. "We will do nothing. Nothing at all."

The pharaoh saw that in spite of his plan his Hebrew slaves continued to grow more numerous. The overseers wondered at the toughness of their slaves. In half the time it had taken to build one pyramid the year before, three great pyramids were finished. "They seem to sprout from the desert sands," the architects whispered as they planned more elaborate royal tombs for the Hebrews to build.

The pharaoh felt fearful as he gazed from his palace window. Without the great energy and broad backs of the Hebrew slaves, his building plans might not be realized. Once again he sent for the midwives.

Shiphrah and Puah paused outside the heavy door to the council chamber. Their hands trembled and their knees quaked. They looked each other in the eye with a steady gaze, each pretending to be brave before the other. But neither woman said a word.

Pharaoh folded his arms across his chest and glared

down at the two women. "How dare you let the boy babies live!" he bellowed. "If my plan to protect Egypt is to succeed, the Hebrew boys must not live."

Puah closed her eyes. She could almost feel the heavy hands of the palace guards dragging her across the cold stone floors of the palace to the filth of the prison house.

Shiphrah stepped forward. "You see, O Pharaoh, the Hebrew women are not like Egyptian women. They give birth to their babies before the midwife can arrive." She bowed low. "It is out of our hands."

Pharaoh scowled and strode over to the window. In the courtyard below, his daughter sat in the shade of a lemon tree. She was plucking the strings of a lyre with her long delicate fingers. Notes of her sweet melody reached her father's ears. "No one has a better daughter than I," he said, his voice suddenly gentle. The midwives hurried from the sight of the ruler, amazed that they had been saved from his wrath.

From that time on, the midwives prospered. Every tree that they planted was studded with plump fruit. Their vines trailed along the ground weighted with melons. Their cows birthed the finest calves. Wearing delicate rings of filigreed gold on every finger, the midwives held the respect of everyone in the country.

And in the fields and on the building sites the Hebrews grew more numerous.

Pharaoh paced the dark palace night after night, wondering what to do. Finally he summoned his advisers. "Listen carefully. This morning I make my

most important decree," he said. "Every newborn son must be exposed on the Nile. But any daughter may live. Command all my people to remain vigilant, to carry out my order."

Now, a woman and her husband from the tribe of Levi lived in bondage in the land of Egypt at the time the pharaoh issued his decree. The Levite woman, who was about to have a baby, watched the soldiers of the pharaoh roaming the countryside, prying into women's workbaskets and under broad watermelon vines—any place they suspected a newly born boy might be hidden. The ruler's men strode rudely through the Hebrews' quarters, listening for the cries of newborn babies. The hills and fields resounded with the groans of families grieving for the babies who had lived only a few days.

The woman Jochebed gave birth to a beautiful baby boy, and whenever she looked at him, she knew that she must protect him from the sharp sword of the pharaoh's anger. Each morning she wondered how she would protect her son from the pharaoh's edict of death.

When the boy was three months old, and his lusty cries could be easily heard, his mother knew that she could not hide him at home any longer. Working in secret, with only her daughter Miriam beside her, Jochebed set out to build a tiny ark of bulrushes to float upon the Nile. She smeared the ark inside and out with pitch and bitumen. She wove the rushes loosely for the cover of the ark so that plenty of air would reach the baby.

When she was satisfied that the small craft was watertight and sturdy, she laid her young son inside his ark and set him in the thick reeds at the shore of the Nile. "Let this ark protect him from the evil that rains all around him," she prayed.

The baby's sister Miriam had gone with her mother to the riverbank that morning. She stood a short distance away to watch what would become of her baby brother. For a while the baby slept, snug within his ark. A gentle current rippled across the river. Miriam continued to wait.

After a while she saw the daughter of Pharaoh with her women attendants coming down to the river to bathe. The attendants chatted to one another while the princess waded into the water.

The next moment Pharaoh's daughter glimpsed the tiny ark caught in a tangle of reeds. "Quick, bring the basket to me," she called to one of her attendants.

The princess leaned over the ark and heard a baby crying. She opened the cover of the ark and gazed at the child lying upon layers of soft cloth kept dry by the skillfully woven basket. She wiped the tears from his face with her delicate hands. "This is a Hebrew baby!" She smoothed his soft cheek. "He is hungry!"

The baby's sister approached the daughter of the pharaoh. "Shall I call a Hebrew nurse for you, one who could care for the baby?" Miriam asked in a strong, clear voice.

The princess looked down at the child. He had fallen asleep in his ark, resting against her sheltering arm. "Yes, that's a wonderful idea." As soon as the

words were out of the princess' mouth, Miriam ran off. Her feet barely touching the ground, she hurried back to the quarters of the Hebrew slaves.

"Mother, come quick! I have orders from the daughter of the pharaoh."

"What has happened, Miriam?" her mother asked. "How can there be more trouble! Has God indeed forsaken our people?"

"Oh, no, Mother. My baby brother shall live."

"Calm yourself, my brave daughter! Speak plainly."

Dancing from foot to foot, Miriam told her mother what had taken place at the bank of the Nile. "She wants to see you right away. You shall nurse the baby. The daughter of the pharaoh has commanded it!"

Mother and daughter hugged and kissed and made their way along the banks of the Nile. Still not believing her good fortune, the Levite woman arrived at the place where the daughter of the pharaoh waited.

"I want you to nurse this child for me," said the princess, waving a pretty feather in front of the smiling infant. "I will pay your wages myself."

Jochebed held her son close to her. Through the blanket she could feel his heart beat in rhythm with her own. "I shall care for him as though he were my own small son," she promised the ruler's daughter.

"And when he is old enough," the princess replied, "I shall raise him as my son. He shall be tutored with my brothers and trained like a true son of the court. He shall be strong and brave, a leader as important in Egypt as the Nile from which he came."

When the boy had outgrown the need of a nurse, his mother and sister were sad in their hearts. But they kept their agreement and left him at the palace with the daughter of Pharaoh. As she had promised, the princess adopted him as her son and gave him a special name.

She called him Moses.

Notes

We have sought to capture the humor of the original story. The Hebrew writer portrays a foolish pharaoh who is anxious about the growing number of Hebrew slaves within his realm, though he would have needed many slaves for his massive building projects. His solutions are clearly short-sighted: hard work does not necessarily solve a population problem, nor is killing babies an answer to an immediate problem. Moreover, cultures that resorted to infanticide to control population killed girls and not boys. This leads us into another theme of the story, the pharaoh's blindness to the power of women. The exodus begins in the disobedience of women: the passive disobedience of the midwives and the active disobedience of Moses' mother and Pharaoh's own daughter! One of the sharpest ironies in the story is the fact that the first person to whom the idea of an exodus occurs is the Egyptian pharaoh, not the Hebrew people.

The biblical story emphasizes the important role of "daughters." The text calls Moses' mother "the daughter of Levi." She and "the daughter of Pharaoh" openly disobey the pharaoh's edict to kill boy babies, and it is "daughters" whose lives Pharaoh is willing to spare.

The use of "ark" rather than the traditional "basket" in our story directs attention to a crucial insight that readers of the Hebrew text would have recognized. The Hebrew word we translate as "ark" appears only twice in the Bible, here and in the story of Noah's ark. The symbolism is evident: whereas Noah's ark saved humanity, Moses' ark saves the future leader of his people. Noah builds the ark that saves creation; Moses' mother builds the ark that saves her people by saving their future leader.

We were unable to capture in English the significance of the pun on the name Moses. The name is Egyptian, meaning "begotten" or "born" (as in Thutmose, Ramses, etc.), but the Hebrew writer wants it understood as a Hebrew name related to the Hebrew word *mashah*, meaning "to draw out." Pharaoh's daughter explains the name as if it means "the one drawn out," i.e., of the water; however, the name Moses, in Hebrew *Moshe*, means "the one who draws out." The special name foreshadows Moses' future role as the one who draws out or leads his people out of bondage in Egypt to the promised land.

THE EXODUS

"Let's hope things turn out better today than yesterday," Aaron said to his brother.

Moses nodded in agreement. "Three days was all we asked the ruler. Three days for the Israelites to go and hold a feast in honor of our God."

Aaron shook his head sadly. "Now our people are worse off than before. Not only must we make the bricks for Pharaoh's building projects, now we must even gather the straw to make the bricks ourselves. Is there no end to the pharaoh's stubbornness?"

"And our own people are blaming us for their new hardships," Moses reminded him. "I heard loud grumbling in the marketplace yesterday when we left the palace."

The two men were on their way to see the pharaoh of Egypt. They hoped this time to convince the ruler to allow the Hebrew people to leave the land of

Egypt. The Lord God had assured Moses that with Aaron's help, Moses would lead the Hebrew people out of Egypt from under Pharaoh's heavy hand. Out of bondage into the promised land, a land flowing with milk and honey.

"When the pharaoh sees the wonders I perform with this staff, he will surely let our people go, as God has commanded, so that we may serve God in the wilderness instead of serving the pharaoh as we have for these past four hundred years."

Aaron put his hand on his brother's shoulder. "We certainly didn't glorify the name of God yesterday. Each wonder we could perform, the pharaoh's wise men matched. Our staff turned into a snake; their staffs turned into snakes. I didn't think they could turn a staff into a snake, but it was child's play for the sorcerer."

"But your staff swallowed up theirs," Moses reminded him. "The Lord God's will is to set us free from bondage. No Pharaoh's wise men are a match for our God. Remember all that God told me on the mountain."

"You have been chosen of all God's people. We must follow the Lord's orders."

Moses noticed that Aaron looked at him with pride. "God commanded me to lead the Hebrew people—I wish some other person had been chosen. I don't speak well, the pharaoh isn't going to listen to me."

"The pharaoh doesn't have to listen to you. He must listen to God. And I shall speak for you when we are in the presence of the pharaoh when your

tongue gets heavy in your mouth." Aaron frowned. "Will I be eloquent enough to describe such wonders as you say the staff can perform?"

Moses shook his head. "I do not say anything. It is God who speaks through me."

Aaron paused at the side of the road and took the staff in his hand. "God will keep the covenant God made with our ancestors. We will come into the good and broad land God promised would be ours. The Lord appeared to Abraham, to Isaac and Jacob, and now —"

"God has appeared to me," Moses said in hushed tones. "And said that today when we stretch the staff over the waters of the Nile, the river will turn to blood."

The brothers went to meet the pharaoh and his magicians at the bank of the Nile. As Pharaoh approached the river, surrounded by his courtiers, the two Israelites grew nervous because the Egyptian magicians displayed such confidence.

Moses addressed the pharaoh in a steady voice. "Why do you refuse to let the Hebrew slaves go to worship the Lord our God in the wilderness?"

The pharaoh and his courtiers laughed.

Moses lifted his staff and struck the water of the Nile, as God had commanded him. Instantly the waters of the Nile ran red with blood. All the waters of Egypt became bloody. There was blood in the canals of the Nile and in the ponds. The fish in the river died and the smell of rotten fish filled the land. People were unable to drink the foul waters of the Nile.

Even the water they had stored in their houses in wooden bowls and stone jars turned to blood.

The Egyptian magicians could perform the same spell and were not impressed.

Pharaoh turned his back on his people and returned to his palace. For seven days the people had to dig deep into the ground near the Nile, searching for water to drink, water that had not been turned to blood.

A week later Moses and Aaron were again on their way to see the pharaoh.

"God has promised, if the pharaoh does not release us from our labors to worship God in the wilderness, frogs will cover the entire land." Aaron turned to Moses. "Imagine a plague of frogs so severe! No one has ever seen such a thing."

Moses laughed and gestured toward the palace in the distance. "Imagine frogs in the palace, frogs in the pharaoh's bed, frogs in the royal ovens where the pharaoh's bread is baked."

"Frogs in the kneading bowls!" Aaron exclaimed.

And it happened exactly as God had said it would. Since the Egyptian magicians could produce frogs in the sandals of the courtiers and entwined in the strings of the musicians' lyres, they were not impressed.

But the pharaoh summoned Moses and Aaron. Shaking a couple of frogs off his arm, he said, "Pray to your God to remove the plague of frogs from the houses and fields of my people, and I'll let your people go to make a sacrifice to your God."

"Tell me the precise time you would like the frogs

to disappear," Moses said, spreading his arms wide and dislodging a group of frogs on a nearby table. "Then you shall see how wondrous is the Lord our God."

It was exactly as Moses had predicted. By nightfall frogs no longer leapt upon the tables and window ledges. But as the people cleaned up their land after the plague, mounds of rotting frogs set up a stench throughout the land.

People put damp cloths over their faces to try to block the revolting odor. "These rotten frogs stink even more than the rotten fish!" they complained. Inside the palace the pharaoh remained stubborn and he refused to allow the Hebrews to go.

The Lord God sent Moses and Aaron to negotiate again. When the pharaoh refused the request of the Hebrews, Aaron smacked the staff into the dust of the earth at Pharaoh's feet and the dust became clouds of mosquitoes throughout the land. The Egyptian magicians cast spell after spell, but they could not match the plague of mosquitoes. No Egyptian sorcerer could produce mosquitoes from dust.

"The finger of God is at work in this," they told the pharaoh, their eyes wide with awe. Forgetting their usual dignity, the magicians begged each other to scratch the bites they couldn't reach.

"Nonsense, it is a spell, like all spells." The pharaoh scratched his ear and went inside his palace.

A fourth time Moses and Aaron were instructed by God to speak to the pharaoh. They set off quite early in the morning to meet the ruler as he was returning to his palace from the river.

The two brothers blocked the path of the pharaoh. "The Lord God says if you do not let us go to prepare a feast to honor God, there will be swarms of flies throughout the land, flies in the fields and in the houses of the Egyptians. Flies will swarm upon you and your people. They will rest upon you thick and heavy as garments of stinging cloth. It will be like nothing you've ever known before. But there will be no flies in the land of Goshen, where the Hebrew slaves live. Tomorrow it will happen just as I say."

The pharaoh said nothing. The next day in all the fields and houses across the land of Egypt flies began to ruin the land. Flies buzzed in the vinegar jars of Egyptian kitchens. Flies crawled in the powder bowls and cosmetic jars of the women of the royal court. Flies crawled upon people's food and even flew into their mouths when they opened them to speak. But in the Hebrews' houses there were no flies.

"Begin the sacrifice to your God," the pharaoh cried to Moses and Aaron.

Moses shook his head. "We cannot sacrifice here where the Egyptian people can see us. Our sacrifices are offensive to your people, and they would stone us to death. We must be allowed to make a three-day journey away from this land into the wilderness to perform our sacrifices and worship our God."

"As long as you don't go too far away," the pharaoh conceded. "Just pray to your God on my behalf that the flies may disappear."

Moses prayed on Pharaoh's behalf as he had agreed to do and the Lord God made the flies disappear. Not

one fly was left anywhere in the land of Egypt. Free of the annoying plague, the pharaoh became stubborn once again. He went back on his word and would not permit the Hebrews to leave their labors.

As Moses and Aaron returned to the palace the next day, their hearts were heavy. "Each of the wonders the Lord God has performed has not changed the pharaoh. Perhaps the pharaoh is too stubborn for the Lord our God."

Moses cried out, "God has promised to deliver us from Egypt, and it will be so. Not when we would have it done, but when God would have it done."

They warned the pharaoh that a terrible plague was about to strike his livestock. The horses, the donkeys, the camels, the cattle, and the sheep—every firstborn animal belonging to the Egyptians—would die if the Hebrews were not freed to worship and perform sacrifices in the wilderness in honor of their God.

"The plague will strike tomorrow, but it will strike only your livestock," Moses assured the pharaoh. "Animals that belong to the Hebrews shall be safe."

It happened as Moses predicted, but the pharaoh remained in his palace. He would not let the Hebrew people go.

Moses and Aaron returned to the pharaoh. Standing directly in front of the ruler, Moses took a handful of soot and threw it into the air. The pharaoh shrugged at Moses' dramatic gesture. Suddenly a fine dust settled over the land. Within a short time boils erupted upon all the living creatures of Egypt. Lambs

lay on the ground and bleated in pain. Pharaoh's fine horses pawed the ground restlessly.

Some Egyptian magicians were so hobbled from the pain of boils on the soles of their feet that they could not appear before Moses to perform wonders of their own. Other sorcerers could not bear to sit because the boils had spread all over their bodies.

The pharaoh was unmoved by the pain all around him. The Lord God had strengthened his resolve.

When Moses and Aaron appeared before the pharaoh again, Moses began to speak at once. "Hear the word of the Lord God. 'Now I shall send all my plagues against you and the people of Egypt. I could have stretched out my hand and destroyed you with plague and pestilence. I could have wiped you from the face of the earth. Do you know why I have spared you? Because I wanted to show you my extraordinary power. I wanted my fame spread far and wide throughout the land. Yet you continue to crush my chosen people. And so tomorrow at this same time I shall send a storm of hail, the likes of which has never been seen or imagined in Egypt. I warn you now. Bring all your livestock into the shelters. All your people must stay in their houses, for the hail will destroy all that it rains upon.' "

When Moses finished speaking, some of the pharaoh's courtiers hurried out of the council chamber to bring their slaves and animals indoors to safety. Others scoffed at the idea. "No one is more powerful than our pharaoh. He too is divine," they said.

The next morning, as God had instructed, Moses

stretched his hands out to the skies. Thunder rolled, lightning blazed like fire, and hail crashed onto every inch of the land of Egypt. Chunks of hail killed all living things that had remained out-of-doors. Trees were snapped from their roots; vines and crops were torn from the ground. Only the land of Goshen, where the Hebrews dwelled, was free of the violent storm.

Pharaoh sent for Moses and Aaron and pleaded with them to intercede with God. All around them the hail continued to pummel the earth. "The Lord is right. I am wrong," the pharaoh cried. "The Hebrews may leave."

"When I have left the city, I shall stretch out my hands and the hail will cease." Moses looked the pharaoh square in the eye. "But I know that you do not truly respect the Lord."

So Moses left the city and stretched out his hands, and the heavy hail stopped. But when Pharaoh saw that the fearsome storm had subsided, he became stubborn and he refused to let the people of Israel leave their labors.

"When will this end, when will we be free?" Aaron wondered aloud.

"This is part of the plan of God," Moses reminded his brother. "So that the Egyptians will know the might and power of God."

Aaron looked up at the sky. The dark gray clouds were pierced with streaks of light. "And what stories we shall tell our children, and their children, and their children! Generation after generation will hear

how the Lord God performed signs more wondrous than the magicians of Egypt and finally outwitted the pharaoh. Only our God could do that!"

"Let's go back and face the pharaoh again," Moses said.

Aaron agreed. "God has seen to it that this storm has passed."

Around the palace the courtiers were discouraged. Glum and exhausted from all the disasters that had befallen them, no one said a word as Moses and Aaron were shown into the presence of Pharaoh.

"If you do not let us go, Pharaoh, the Lord God is going to send locusts into your country. They shall cover the land like a crust. Not a leaf or stone shall be visible. Whatever was left after the hailstorm shall be eaten by the locusts. Not a turnip or an onion or a leek shall remain in the fields. Then the locusts shall attack the houses; they shall infest the bedlinens and the clothing of every Egyptian, from the richest of your advisers to the poorest farmer. Nothing like this plague has been seen or heard of in the whole history of Egypt."

Moses and Aaron did not wait for an answer, but left the pharaoh and his advisers to think over all the Lord God had said.

The advisers gathered around the pharaoh and did not wait for permission to speak. "This man is ruining Egypt. You must let them go and worship their God. Before everything in Egypt is as lifeless as the stalks of corn rotting on the ground."

"Yes, yes, I shall let them go," the pharaoh ex-

claimed and sent for Moses and Aaron, who were waiting in the courtyard. "If I let your people go, who exactly shall make this trip into the wilderness?"

Moses answered without delay. "Everyone, young and old alike, must go. Our daughters and our sons. Our flocks and herds. We must all attend this special feast to the Lord."

"You think I am foolish? Let the children go with you? What kind of evil plan do you have in mind, Moses! The men may go to make the sacrifice. But all the rest will stay behind. Now get out of my sight!"

So Moses stretched his staff over the land of Egypt and the Lord drove an east wind over the land all that day and all that night. When morning came, the locusts had blackened every inch of the land. Not a shred of green plant or leaf or bud was left anywhere in Egypt.

At last the pharaoh was stunned. He summoned Moses and Aaron. "I have sinned against the Lord your God and against you. Now forgive me, please. Intercede just this once with your God so that this wretched plague will be lifted."

Moses interceded and the Lord answered with a mighty west wind that swept the locusts into the sea. As soon as the last of the insects had been blown away from the land, the Lord strengthened Pharaoh's resolve and he forbade the Hebrews to leave the land.

When Moses stretched out his head toward the skies the next morning, darkness fell on the land. For three days the darkness was so thick that mothers could not see their children; farmers could not find

their flocks. People remained in their houses, howling in fear.

But the Hebrews had light where they lived and were not afraid.

"All right, you may go, even your children may go, but the flocks and herds shall remain behind," Pharaoh said to Moses.

"Our livestock must go with us, for we shall need them in order to have animals that we can sacrifice to the Lord our God. We shall not leave behind one single lamb."

"Get out of my sight," the pharaoh thundered, hurling a terra-cotta fish to the floor. "I never want to see you in my presence again, Moses!"

Moses and Aaron left the palace, their hearts trembling. They had performed the Lord's wonders before Pharaoh, his magicians, and his advisers. But the Lord had made Pharaoh stubborn so that he would not allow the Israelites to leave the land. Now the time had come for the Lord God to perform the sign that would set the people of Israel free of their long bondage.

Moses appeared before the pharaoh to report the words of the Lord. "At midnight I shall go forth among the Egyptians, and every firstborn in the land of Egypt shall die, from your own firstborn, Pharaoh, who is in line to succeed you on the throne of Egypt, to the firstborn of the poorest young woman grinding flour on the millstone."

Pharaoh said nothing. His hands remained lifeless in his lap. Moses continued. "There shall be a great

cry in the land as Egyptian babies die. But among God's chosen people, not a single infant shall be harmed. You shall know the power of the Lord God and all your people shall honor me. Then shall I and all the Hebrew people leave the land."

And Moses turned and left the presence of the pharaoh.

The Hebrews did as Moses had ordered them. They smeared blood from the passover sacrifice onto the lintels and doorposts of their houses. They gathered their possessions and their flocks and prepared to leave the land of Egypt.

At midnight the Lord God killed all the firstborn in Egypt. In the palace the son of Pharaoh, the young boy who someday would have ruled over the land, lay dead. In the fields the firstborn of every cow and sheep and camel was struck down. Even the first-born of the prisoner in the jail died during that dark night. But the angel of death passed over the houses of the Hebrews.

The people of Egypt wailed in grief, for no house in Egypt was without its dead. In the midst of the terror, Pharaoh sent for Moses and Aaron. "Get away from our land, you and all your people. Take your children and herds and go to offer sacrifice to your God. And ask a blessing for me also, for I lost my firstborn son this night."

Later, when Pharaoh heard that the Hebrews had actually made their exodus, he and his advisers changed their minds about letting their slaves depart from the

land of Egypt. "What have we done, allowing our best workers to leave our service?" the pharaoh shouted to his courtiers.

The men looked at each other and bowed low before their leader. "Command us and we shall bring back those Hebrews!" they vowed.

'Take six hundred of our best chariots; gather the troops! We shall chase the Hebrews across the wilderness; we shall bring them back. Everything in the land shall be just as it was before Moses performed his many signs for their God."

The Israelites, together with their children and flocks and herds, were making their way through the night. They had left in such haste that the dough was still warm in the kneading bowls. When they reached the sea and could go no farther, they saw Pharaoh and his soldiers gaining on them.

The Hebrews were terrified at the sight of the Egyptians in their gleaming chariots. "What have you done to us, Moses? Weren't there graves in Egypt wide enough to hold us? Why did you bring us to the wilderness to die before the wrath of Pharaoh!"

Moses tried to calm the people, but it was of no use. The complaints rained around him. "We would rather make bricks for the overseers in Egypt than be slaughtered by them in the wilderness."

Moses raised his rod over his head. When the people were silent, he spoke. "Have you forgotten that God is with us? God has brought us from the crushing hand of Pharaoh. God has heard our cries.

God will wrestle with the pharaoh, God will stand in the path of the angry horses. God will fight for us."

Then, as the Lord God commanded, Moses took his staff and stretched out his hand over the sea. The waters rolled up on each side so that the Israelites were able to walk across the floor of the sea as though it were dry land.

Seeing the path cut deep into the sea, the pharaoh urged his charioteer to gallop forward at top speed. "We shall overtake those Hebrews, and they shall learn who is master."

As the charioteers followed their leader into the sea, the mighty waters rolled back into the path, swallowing the Egyptians. As the Israelites glanced back over their shoulders they saw the sea, spread deep and wide all around them. Not a single Egyptian remained alive.

Miriam the prophet stood at the shore with the other Hebrew leaders. As the women danced with timbrels, Miriam's voice rang out across the sea.

> *"Sing to the Lord, who has triumphed gloriously;*
> *Horse and rider are thrown into the sea."*

The Israelites were astounded by the victory of the Lord God. They had been rescued from the land of Egypt as God had promised. Their God had triumphed over the power of the mighty pharaoh. They worshiped God, and led by Moses, Miriam, and Aaron, the people of Israel set out on the journey that would

take them to the promised land. All the way Miriam's song accompanied them.

"You will bring them and plant them
On the mountain of your heritage,
The place of your dwelling
Which you have established, O Lord."

Notes

The story of the ten plagues shows the struggle between two rival powers, the God of Israel and the pharaoh of Egypt. For the biblical writers it is no real contest. The power of Israel's God over Pharaoh, whom the Egyptians regarded as divine, is demonstrated not only by Pharaoh's helplessness in the face of the plagues but also by the repeated motif of God strengthening Pharaoh's resolve. Numerous Bible translations render this motif literally as "God hardened the heart of Pharaoh" or "Pharaoh hardened his heart." Since in Hebrew thought, the heart is the seat of the intellect and the will—and not, as we tend to think of it, the place of emotions and feelings—we have interpreted this phrase in its intended sense, as stubbornness or as God strengthening Pharaoh's resolve.

THE

PROMISED LAND

Moses was one hundred and twenty years old. He had led the Israelites through the wilderness for forty years. He had encouraged them when they were low, had given them strength when they were weak. He had spoken the words of the Lord to them many times. Each time they forgot their promises to God, Moses again recited to them the blessings and curses that would result from their actions.

"The Lord is delivering us from the cruel whips of Pharaoh. The Lord is going to lead us this night out of Egypt," Moses had cried the night the Lord God smote the firstborn of all Egyptians.

"On these tablets are written the commandments and teachings of the Lord," Moses had proclaimed to them at Sinai. There on the top of the mountain the glory of the Lord had appeared like a devouring

fire. Moses went up the mountain and remained there with the Lord for forty days and forty nights.

His face burning from having seen the Lord God face-to-face, Moses had come down the mountain and rejoined the people. "We must make an ark of wood and put the tablets bearing the words of the Lord inside it. The ark shall travel with us from now on." With the ark containing the testimony of the Lord before them, Moses and his sister Miriam and his brother Aaron led the people wherever the Lord commanded. Year after year, following the pillar of cloud by day and the pillar of fire by night, they made their way through the desert wilderness.

Finally having reached the plains of Moab, Moses called the people together. "Now the time has come for you to take possession of the land that the Lord God has promised you. Now you will enter the rich land that lies beyond the Jordan River. But my feet will never tread that ground. My eyes have seen the valleys and the mountain ranges from the top of Mount Pisgah, but the Lord has decided that I may not cross over into the land. For I angered the Lord at Meribah, and God would not hear my pleas to be allowed to go with you. I angered the Lord for your sakes, and now I shall not go into the promised land."

The people left Moses alone on the mountainside, where he was preparing to die. He watched as the people went about their daily tasks, and he remembered times of hardships and joys while he had led the Israelites through the wilderness. Only he had been allowed to see the Lord face-to-face, to perform

the signs and wonders of the Lord God of Israel before the pharaoh of Egypt and before God's chosen people.

Moses thought of the time his sister Miriam had grown angry with him. "Why should he be the only one to speak the words of the Lord God?" she had complained. God had punished Miriam for speaking against him. In an instant her skin had turned white as snow. For seven days she had been required to remain outside the camp. The people refused to continue their journey until she had been healed of her punishment. They had loved Miriam, as much as he had himself. How splendid she had been the day she sang the people across the sea. He would never forget her words.

> *Sing to the Lord, who has triumphed gloriously;*
> *Horse and rider are thrown into the sea.*

How long the journey had seemed. They had been traveling for many months and the people were tired of the manna the Lord had provided them to eat. Each day they gathered just enough of the honeylike substance to feed themselves and their families. "Never gather more than you can eat in one day," the Lord God had commanded. And indeed as the Lord had warned, the extra manna spoiled in the hands of the greedy.

"Meat, the people want meat." Moses tried to intercede with the Lord. "How can I continue to lead this stiff-necked people, Lord? I am tired of nursing them, tending to all their needs. How can I be mother

to six hundred thousand? I am not able to bear this people alone."

Now when Moses thought about the wanderings in the wilderness, the time seemed short. But when he looked out over the settlement, the task seemed far from finished.

God spoke to Moses on the mountain. "Soon you will sleep with your ancestors. And this people you have led for so long through the wilderness, this people will go astray and will forsake me, and they will break the covenant I have made with them. I shall bring them into the land of milk and honey, and after they have fed themselves and grown fat, they will worship other gods, and I shall hide my face from them. So write all that I have told you in this book, Moses, to serve as my witness, so that the children of the children of Israel shall not forget."

Moses did as the Lord commanded him. "Take this book containing the Lord's teaching," he told the priests, "and place it inside the ark of the covenant. Gather to me all the people that I may speak to them one last time."

Moses gathered his strength and stood before the people. "You have rebelled against God while I have been alive. How much more so after my death? People of Israel, listen to my words. You must love the Lord your God with your whole being."

Then Moses turned to Joshua and spoke to him one final time.

"Be strong and of good courage, Joshua, son of Nun. For now you shall bring the Israelites into the

land. The Lord God will go before you and will not forsake you. Do not be afraid, for the Lord God will be with you."

Then Moses died as the Lord had decreed. God buried him in the land of Moab and to this day no one knows where his grave is. The Israelites wept for Moses for thirty days. When the days of mourning were finished, Joshua, the son of Nun, led the people into the promised land.

To prepare for their entry into the land on the other side of the Jordan River, Joshua sent out two spies secretly to bring back reports about the land surrounding Jericho. When the men reached the walls of the city of Jericho, they stopped for the night at the house of Rahab. Almost immediately word reached the king of Jericho that two Israelites were there, intending to spy out the country.

The king sent messengers to Rahab ordering her to turn over the Israelite spies. "We have come for the men who came to spend the night in your house. We have learned that they are here to spy out our country."

Rahab looked at the messengers levelly. "Yes, they were here," she replied calmly, "but they left a while ago. I did not know where they had come from. They left just as the time approached for the city gates to be closed for the night. Since they have not been traveling long, if you leave now, you will surely be able to catch up with them."

The messengers hurried off, and the city gates were

closed behind them. They traveled as far as the banks of the Jordan but saw no sign of the Israelite men.

When the king's men had gone, Rahab went up to the roof of her house, which was built into the wall of the city. There, hidden among stalks of flax, were the two Israelites.

"I know that the Lord God has given this land to you. We have all heard how the Lord dried up the waters of the sea when you were fleeing the Egyptian persecutors." Rahab took a handful of flax and began to braid it as she talked. "I know that the Lord God is God over all heaven and earth. Since I have spared your lives, swear to me by your God that you will keep faith with my family."

The men stood up, shaking the long husks of flax from their limbs. "Our lives for yours, so long as you do not reveal our business."

Rahab was not yet satisfied. "Give me a token of your faith. I must be sure that you will spare my father and mother, brothers and sisters, when you descend upon Jericho."

The first man stepped forward. "When the Lord God delivers this land into our hands, we will certainly deal faithfully with you and your family."

Rahab dropped a thick rope of hemp through an opening in the roof so that the men could climb down the wall outside the city.

"Hide in the hills for three days," she told them. "By that time your pursuers will have given up the chase. They will return to the city, and then you will be safe to go on your way."

The men looked up at the beautiful woman who had risked so much for them. "As soon as you see us enter the land, hang a scarlet cord in this opening in the roof, where the rope now hangs. Make sure that your entire family is inside the house with you. If any of them is outside in the street or is in another house, their life will not be long. But if any of our soldiers touches you or anyone in your house, then the guilt will be upon our heads."

The men jumped from the rope onto the ground below. "If you tell anyone where we are hiding, then you will die alongside everyone else in Jericho."

Rahab watched until the men were out of sight. Then she tied a slender scarlet cord to the opening in her roof. When the king's guards returned to the city without finding the spies, the king ordered that the gates of the city be bolted. All the people of Jericho remained inside the thick city walls. The door of every house was barred. The people of Jericho waited in fear. Rahab watched from her window for the Israelites to cross the Jordan.

Joshua and the Israelites encamped for three days on the banks of the Jordan. It was the time of the harvest, and the river was at flood stage. While the people waited for the spies to return from Jericho, children played along the riverbank. Women danced and men relaxed, trying not to think of the fierce battle ahead.

Joshua arose early before the people were stirring. He looked across the river to the land of Jericho and

remembered the long wanderings of the Israelites. That morning the Lord said to Joshua, "Today I shall begin to make you great in the eyes of the people. Just as I was with Moses, now I shall be with you. So command the priests who carry the ark of the covenant to bear the ark before the people into the river."

When Joshua gathered the priests and all the Israelites that morning, he told them what the Lord had commanded them to do. They looked at their leader in wonder. "How shall we stand in the river, carrying the ark aloft?" asked the priests.

"You must stand in the word of the Lord," Joshua told them.

"Now, people of Israel, you will know today that the living God is among you. Every one of you will pass before the ark and cross the Jordan, and wait on the other side of the river. Then the priests will pass before you, carrying the ark."

The people looked with disbelief at the swift current of the Jordan.

Suddenly, as soon as the soles of the feet of the priests were standing in the waters of the Jordan River, the waters rolled back. And all the day long while the people of each of the twelve tribes were passing through the dry riverbed of the Jordan, the water did not flow in or out of the Jordan. As the Lord God had promised, the waters were piled up on both sides of the Jordan and no water flowed from the Jordan into the Dead Sea.

"We were standing in the river and our feet are

dry," the people marveled. "All that you command us to do, Joshua, we shall do!"

As soon as the soles of the feet of the priests were once again on dry land, the waters of the Jordan rushed into the riverbed. The people stood silently as the priests bore the ark of the covenant ahead of them toward Jericho. And the river Jordan overflowed its banks because it was the time of harvest.

Notes

Moses holds a special place in Israelite tradition. As leader, lawgiver, and prophet, he dominates the biblical narrative of Exodus, Leviticus, Numbers, and Deuteronomy. Even Moses, however, is not portrayed as a perfect human being. He is not permitted to enter the promised land with the people he led through the desert wilderness for forty years. Why? The book of Deuteronomy blames the people's sin; Numbers suggests that Moses showed lack of faith.

His death, like his birth, is unusual. He lives the ideal life span of one hundred and twenty years with no signs of aging. God buries him and no one knows the site of his grave.

Joshua appears in the biblical story as a second Moses, performing many of the deeds Moses had performed. As Moses' divinely designated successor, Joshua leads the Israelites across the Jordan River just as Moses had led them across the sea when they were fleeing from the Egyptians. In both accounts God dries up the water, allowing the chosen people to effect a seemingly impossible crossing.

The ark of the covenant is transported with the Israelites

to serve as a sign of the presence of God in their midst throughout the journey to the promised land.

In ancient Palestine the walled city served as protection against enemy attack. People left the city early in the morning to work the surrounding fields and returned in the evening to their homes inside the fortified city. The city gates were then closed for the night. According to the sixth chapter of the book of Joshua, the Israelites do not take the city of Jericho by force but rather through a ritual ceremony that causes the walls to tumble down.

The two men Joshua sends to Jericho were not particularly good spies, since their presence quickly became known. The story stresses Rahab's role in protecting them and her family. A non-Israelite, she testifies to the power of Israel's God and allies herself with the chosen people. In rabbinic tradition, Rahab is considered one of the four most beautiful women in the world. She is also described as the ancestor of eight prophets, including Jeremiah and Huldah.

DEBORAH,
JUDGE OVER ISRAEL

In the days when Israel had no king, each tribe tried to govern itself. Life was hard; not all the land was fertile for farming and suitable for raising flocks. The Israelites and their neighbors fought over the choice pieces of land. From time to time, a leader appeared who united a few of the tribes in the north in battle against their enemies. But discord was the only steady ruler in the land.

Such disorder brought great trouble to the people. Travelers were attacked by bands of robbers on the roads. Traders were afraid to follow caravan routes, for no one could assure their safety. The Canaanite king Jabin oppressed the people of the central hill country with burdensome taxes. Year after year he took more of their rich farmland, driving the farmers into the rocky hillsides, where few crops thrived.

When the people thought they were beaten, and

had stopped hoping for deliverance from the Canaanite overlords, a woman appeared to shake the people free of their oppression. Deborah, a prophet and a judge over Israel, knew that to repel the forces of King Jabin and his military general, Sisera, the people must be united.

Deborah had gained a reputation as a just and wise judge. Even those against whom she had ruled respected her decisions. People brought her the most difficult disputes, ones that could not be resolved by the elders who sat at the city gates to hear legal arguments.

Deborah lived between the villages of Ramah and Bethel. Day after day she sat under a palm tree and listened to the people of Israel. She heard a farmer accuse his neighbor of planting crops during the times he was required to let his field lie fallow. She determined on whose land disputed vineyards grew. And on some days she heard a sound of the dispute before the two angry people arrived at her spot. Their voices carried down the hillsides while Deborah waited in the morning sunlight to untangle whatever knot would soon be thrown at her feet. And surprisingly no one left her presence feeling worse than when they had arrived.

For some time people had come to Deborah under her palm tree, bringing stories of hardships suffered under King Jabin, who reigned in Hazor. Brought low by the pains of the people, Deborah went off by herself to listen for the voice of God. She wondered how she could ever hope to unite these people who

fought with one another instead of against their common enemy. She called upon the Lord to send her wise counsel. And she waited.

When she returned to her village, she was full of purpose. Immediately she sent for Barak, a brave warrior who would make a good general. "You must go at once, Barak, and assemble ten contingents of men at Mount Tabor."

"Ten contingents? That's not possible," he replied.

"From your own tribe of Naphtali and from Zebulon they will come," she said without hesitation. "The Lord God of Israel will draw out Sisera, the general of Jabin's mighty army, to fight against you in the plain below."

"But he has nine hundred chariots outfitted with iron. We have none."

Deborah continued as though Barak had voiced no objection. "God will send Sisera to meet you on the plain of Esdraelon near the Kishon River. In spite of his nine hundred chariots, in spite of his legions of troops, the victory shall be yours. For the Lord God of Israel will deliver him into your hands."

"If you will go with me, to strengthen me, then I shall do all that you have said. But if you will not be by my side, I cannot lead our troops against such a mighty foe."

"I shall be with you all the time. What is more important, the Lord God shall be with us. We shall call up all the tribes of Israel against the Canaanites. We shall meet the enemy together." Deborah was as calm in the face of the enemy as Barak was con-

cerned. "But you should know that the victory at Esdraelon will not be yours. God intends to deliver Sisera into the hands of a woman."

The general looked at Deborah with increased respect. "The glory shall be yours; I give my vow that everyone shall know the battle was won through the leadership of Deborah."

Deborah spoke no more that day.

> *Hear, O kings and queens, hear our song and remember*
> *The day the leaders became proud in Israel.*
> *When Deborah arose and sang her brave song,*
> *Deborah the prophet called Israel to arms,*
> *Deborah arose and sang her song of victory,*
> *Her song that stirred Barak and the people from*
>   *their fields.*
> *Give your heart to the leaders of Israel,*
> *To Deborah, who leads Israel into battle against*
>   *Sisera.*
> *Hear our joyous melody to the Lord God of Israel.*

Deborah sat on a low stone wall and gazed at the sun-dappled hillside. Its quiet peace was shattered by scores of men hurrying down every path, their cloaks billowing out behind them. Shepherd boys tending their flocks waved as the men passed, on their way to join Barak, answering the call to fight against Sisera in the plain of Esdraelon.

Deborah felt a moment of sadness. Some of the men would never again run down these paths past the olive trees and grape arbors familiar since their youth.

She sought out Barak to report that the tribes of Naphtali and Zebulon were responding with open hearts to the call of God.

A runner had just returned with news for the commander from the settlement of Dan. "The men of Dan cannot leave their work," he reported. "It is the same with the tribes of Asher and Reuben."

Barak ordered that food be brought to the runner and then sent the exhausted man off to rest. He looked up at Deborah. "How will we raise ten contingents of troops to defeat the Canaanite Jabin?"

"Wait," replied the prophet without hesitation. "Wait upon the Lord."

As she spoke, Barak was reminded of her sitting contentedly under the broad leaves of her palm tree, day after day, bringing order and justice to the people who depended on her.

"Without you to guide my step, this battle could not be won," he told her, as he had each day since they had begun to summon the men away from their work in the fields to do battle against Sisera.

"I look forward to the day when the people are at peace and I can return to the quiet of my palm tree, after the battle is won."

> *From Ephraim they set out, farmers into the valley,*
> *Following you, Benjamin, you and your relations.*
> *From Machir marched down eager commanders*
> *And from Zebulon young men carrying their weapons.*
> *The princes of Issachar are with Deborah,*
> *Issachar so faithful to Barak,*

Rushed into battle in the valley,
Close behind Barak and Deborah, resolved to fight
    Sisera
On the heights of the field that day.

Who stopped among the sheepfolds
To listen for children's piping the flocks?
Among the clans of Reuben were great searchings of
    heart.
Gilead stayed on the far bank of the Jordan
And did not cross over to help their neighbors in
    battle.
And Dan chose to sit among their ships.
Asher sat in safety on the coast of the sea
While their neighbors died on the plains,
By their familiar landings they stayed.
But the people Zebulon joined their lives to death;
Naphtali too resolved to fight Sisera
On the heights of the fields that day.

When Sisera heard that Barak had amassed the Israelites at Mount Tabor, the Canaanite general ordered his invincible chariots of iron and every able-bodied man in his army to march with him to the Kishon River.

"This day our iron chariots shall ride over Barak and the Israelite foot soldiers, like rocks crushing clay pots," Sisera assured his restless legions.

When Barak saw the helmets of the hordes of Canaanites gleaming like a solid sheet of metal across the valley, he looked in alarm at his hastily raised army.

"Deborah, are you certain this battle is the will of our God?"

"Hurry, give the call to advance," she responded. "This is the day the Lord has chosen to give Sisera's forces into your hands on the battlefield below."

Barak raised his arm. "The Lord God goes before us," he shouted. And the men charged behind him, down the mountain to meet the iron army of the Canaanite Sisera.

And it was just as Deborah had prophesied. Sisera's chariots of iron became bogged down in the Kishon's muddy waters, and his army fell before the narrow blades of the Israelite swords. Seeing that no chariot remained standing, Sisera fled into the hills on foot.

> *When the Lord went forth in battle*
> *The earth trembled and the mountains quaked*
> *And the iron chariots of Canaan*
> *Collapsed before the power of the Lord.*

Sisera ran through the barren countryside, his garments caked with the dirt of the day. The grit of battle was ground into his skin. He paused at a certain tent, which belonged to the Kenites, a clan who had made a peace treaty with King Jabin. Out of the tent came a woman, smiling welcome.

Since Jael was a Kenite woman, Sisera decided it was safe to stop with her and rest. She would do him no harm.

She seemed to recognize him. "Come in, my Lord, do not be afraid."

"Yes, I will rest here for a moment," he said gratefully. He followed Jael into the cool darkness of the tent. "Please, bring me some water. The day's dour battle lies dry as dust upon my tongue."

Instead of water, she brought him rich milk to drink and she offered him curds in a lordly bowl of silver.

"Please stand watch at the entrance of the tent," he said. "If a soldier comes and asks if there is anyone inside your tent, you must say no."

"Go to sleep now. I will guard you." She covered him and made him comfortable in her tent.

When his eyelids had closed, she walked lightly across the floor. In one graceful movement, she stooped and closed her hand around the heavy tent peg, lying at the edge of her tent.

In her left hand she took a tent peg
And with her right hand she hefted her mallet,
The mallet she used by day to make fast her tent.
She struck Sisera one blow,
Her hammer crushed his head.
He sank, he fell, he lay still at her feet.
Where he sank, there he fell dead.

The mother of Sisera stood at her window
Watching the sunlight fade from the sky.
"This is the day my son crushed the enemy,
Fought them at Taanach by the waters of Megiddo,
Fought them and left them all dead.
Soon he'll ride home with spoils from the battle;

*Embroidered cloth he'll bring me, bright beads for
my neck."*

And so, as the Lord God determined, the people of Israel were victorious over their Canaanite enemy. At the end of that long day, Jabin's forces were destroyed and the people of Israel were delivered from the oppression of his rule.

*Then as Barak had vowed to Deborah
The people raised their voices in triumphant song.
In praise of the prophet who judged Israel,
Deborah, who united her people.
Following God's words, bright as the sun,
She led her people to victory.
Deborah became a hero in Israel
For enflaming the people when their hearts had grown
    cool.*

*The villages in Israel were no more,
They were no more until you arose, Deborah,
Until you arose, leader of Israel.
Come forth now and sing your song to God.*

Notes

The book of Judges contains two accounts of Deborah's victory over the Canaanites, a prose version in chapter 4 and a poetic version in chapter 5. The poem of chapter 5, known as the Song of Deborah, is one of the oldest literary units in the Bible. We have combined the two accounts to

resemble a ballad, since the original song recounts the heroic deeds of Deborah and the tribes of Israel.

In contrast to other battles in the book of Judges, where Israel defends its territory against its hostile neighbors, in this battle Israel fights the Canaanites in the plain, where they had a clear military advantage, not only in troops but also in their use of chariots outfitted with iron.

A military alliance between Jabin and the Kenites explains Sisera's willingness to seek protection from Jael. The fact that the Kenites were related to the Israelites through Moses' father-in-law may have motivated Jael. She was probably skilled in wielding the tent peg and hammer, since pitching the tent was likely women's work, as it still is among the Bedouin today.

JOTHAM'S FABLE

Once upon a time the cedars of Lebanon decided they wanted a strong and wise monarch to rule over them.

"Perhaps I might be king?" asked a young cedar as the sun's rays spread across the pale morning sky.

"What do you know that we do not know? You cast the same shade and bend your limbs to ride the wind just as we do," answered the cedars who stood around it. "Our ruler must be remarkable."

"Perhaps I might be the ruler?" An older cedar tossed its top branches to get their attention. "I am different from the young cedar, for I wonder about things."

"What do you know that we do not know?"

"I know that the sun must go somewhere when it leaves us in the dark. Perhaps there is one special hillside where the great sun spreads its light and warmth without pause. I would like to take root in such a place."

"Our ruler should know precisely where the sun goes!"

The cedars grew excited. "Let us go and find ourselves a ruler!"

Not far away on a nearby hillside grew an olive tree. "See how different that tree is from us!" exclaimed one of the cedars. "We are tall and cast spare shade. But the olive tree is round—and its leaves tremble in the barest breath of air."

"It's the one to be our ruler," they all agreed.

So the dark green cedars approached the gray-green olive tree.

"We are looking for a regent and think that you might be the perfect tree to rule over us."

The olive tree stretched its deeply curved branches to catch a puff of wind. Its fragile leaves stirred. The cedars' branches were too thick to catch such a whisper of wind. "We have chosen well," they assured one another.

Then the olive tree spoke. "Shall I leave my fatness, the prized oil by which gods and people are honored, merely to hold sway over the trees? From the first pressing of my olives comes the finest oil used to anoint leaders. The wealthy covet such oil to refresh and soothe their bodies. And from the second pressing comes oil for cooking and for seasoning food. And don't forget that without my oil, lamps would stand dark and useless."

"Do you scorn the honor of ruling all the trees on the hillside merely to lord over the kitchens of gods and people?"

The cedars raised their branches and scanned the hillside. Growing near a low rocky ledge was a fig tree. "Look, its broad-notched leaves gleam in the sun. Not for us the frail leaves of the olive tree."

The cedars dispatched a delegation to the fig tree. "We saw that your roots wrap around the rocks as though they were kneading rich soil. We must have a powerful tree like you to reign over us."

All along the fig tree's dark branches clung plump fruit. The fig tree sighed, its lowest branches sweeping dust from the rocks at its feet. "Shall I leave my sweetness and my good fruit to hold sway over the other trees?"

"Perhaps we should try the vine?" the cedars wondered. "It winds itself along the arbor and spills down the hillside."

"Yes, the vine, laden with specially honored grapes, is the one we want," clamored the cedars at once.

But the vine would not hear their speech. "Shall I leave my rich red wine, which cheers gods and people and marks their celebrations, to hold sway over the trees?"

"Yes!" cried the cedars, their somber branches so dark next to the lacy vine. But they pleaded in vain with the vine.

Nearby in the white-hot heat of the noonday sun a spiky bramble stood. It looked like a collection of broken sticks tied together with long pieces of dried grass.

"What about you?" the cedars asked the bramble. "Would you be our ruler?"

The bramble, who had heard all that happened on the hillside that morning, looked up into the tallest reaches of the cedars.

"If in good faith you intend to anoint me ruler, then come and let my shade protect you. But if you do not grant me the respect and honor a ruler deserves, then may fire burst out of me and consume all you foolish cedars of Lebanon."

Notes

This fable appears in the Book of Judges, chapter 9. It is one of only two examples of fable in the Bible; the other occurs in 2 Kings 14:9 and is repeated in 2 Chronicles 25:18. The fable of the trees seeking a king is told by Jotham, the youngest son of Gideon. Jotham's half brother Abimelech has just murdered the other sons of Gideon and had himself proclaimed king. Jotham's fable is antimonarchal, and certainly anti-Abimelech. It illustrates the folly of monarchy—only the worst and least qualified aspire to the office—and warns of its dangers: it destroys those who place their reliance on it. The bramble's speech is ironic; it has no shade to offer. It is, however, a likely place for fire to break out.

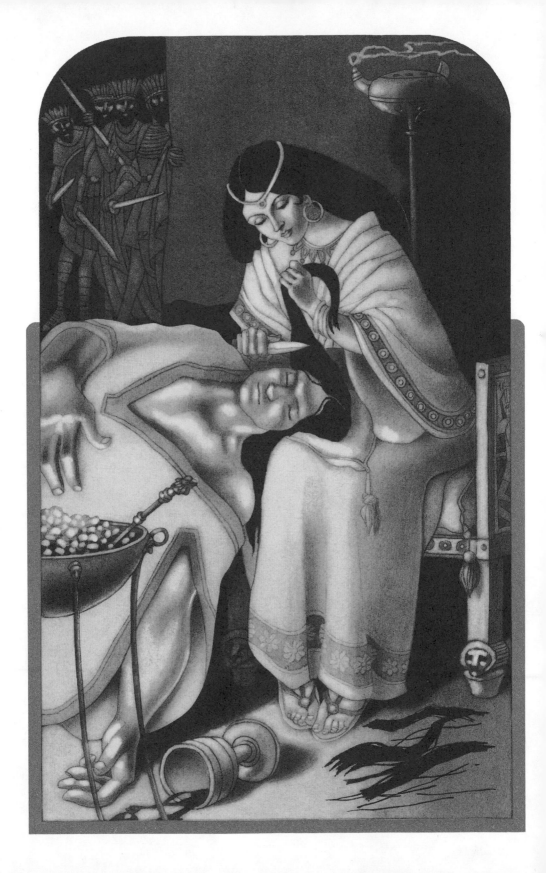

THE ADVENTURES
OF SAMSON

◆◆ That's the woman for
me," thought Samson. "She's the one I want to
marry." He was on his way home from the Philistine
town of Timnah to tell his parents about a young
woman he had seen, helping her mother at the
marketplace.

Upon reaching the settlement of the tribe of Dan,
Samson rushed to find his parents. "This morning in
Timnah I saw a woman I want to marry. Make the
arrangements," Samson demanded. In those times parents arranged marriages for their children.

"Have you been out in the sun too long? You have
lost your reason," they gasped in unison. "Marry a
Philistine woman? You know Israelites and Philistines don't mix. The land is so crowded now we
Israelites hardly have enough fields for grazing our
flocks and planting our crops! And the wily Philistines grab more and more of the fertile plains God

promised to our ancestors. Why can't you marry a nice Israelite woman?"

Samson ignored their question. His parents were baffled. "Our own good son wanting to marry a Philistine!" Manoah complained to his wife. "I can't make such arrangements with a perfidious Philistine."

She shook her head in dismay. "Perhaps he can be persuaded that to marry one of them would be like asking figs from an olive tree."

Later that day Samson's mother approached her son, who was in the field, listening to the crickets' evening song.

"You must listen to me, son," she began in a pleading tone. "God promised us a son who would deliver our people from the Philistines. Since birth you have been dedicated to God as a Nazirite." She touched his head. "Never has your hair been cut. Never have you eaten food forbidden to a Nazirite. Your lips have never touched wine or beer, just as God's messenger commanded me before you were born. And for what? To marry a Philistine? This is how you will deliver our people?"

Her pleading went in vain. Samson clamped his lips together in a look his mother had known since he was a small boy. Sooner or later he would have his way.

"He won't change his mind," she reported to her husband.

But Samson's parents did not know that Samson's folly was part of God's plan. For God was waiting for the right moment to get the better of the Philistines.

A few days later Samson set out for Timnah with his father and mother. They walked so slowly that Samson ran far ahead of them, anxious to show his parents the woman he would marry.

Following a crude path that wound through the vineyards of Timnah, Samson heard a rustling in the undergrowth, then a growl. As he looked up, a young lion, its teeth bared, sprang from behind a rock. Samson grabbed the animal with his bare hands and tore it apart as easily as if he were tearing wheat from the shaft. When he rejoined his parents on the main road, he did not mention what had happened.

Some days later, Samson decided to return to Timnah alone to see the young woman. "I think I'll look and see if the lion's body is still there," he thought. He left the main road and reached the place where he had killed the lion. A swarm of bees had made their nest in the lion's body. "Honey!" exclaimed Samson. "I love honey." And he scooped it out by the handful, ignoring the angry bees all around him. "I'll take some to my parents, but I won't tell them where I found it."

Samson's parents finally agreed to their son's wish to marry a Philistine. Reluctantly Manoah went to Timnah to arrange the marriage. It was the custom for the bridegroom to provide the wedding feast, which would last for an entire week. Thirty young men had been selected from the village to be the groom's attendants. Huge platters of cakes and other sweet delicacies were prepared. Vats of wine were opened. Everyone was in high spirits.

The crowd of Philistine men put Samson in a mischievous mood. "Let's play a game," he said to his thirty guests. "I'll tell you a riddle. If you can guess the answer during the seven days of celebration, I will give you each a fine linen garment. But if you can't guess the answer to my riddle, you must give me thirty fine linen garments."

The Philistines enjoyed contests of wits. They were confident that thirty of them could outwit a single Israelite — even an Israelite reputed to be as clever as Samson.

"Let's hear it! You'd better start looking for those linen garments, Samson!"

The bridegroom looked around at the thirty expectant faces. "They'll never figure it out," he thought. "I've won already!"

Samson cleared his throat and waited until the men were silent.

"Out of the eater came something to eat,
Out of the strong came something sweet."

The Philistines looked at one another, clearly puzzled. They went off into little groups and suggested possible answers.

"Perhaps it's a sheep," one of them volunteered. "A sheep eats and from a sheep we get cheese and milk and yogurt."

"But cheese and milk and yogurt are not sweet. The riddle says sweet."

"What about a fig tree? It's strong. It can survive the long dry summers. And it produces sweet fruit to eat."

"But a tree doesn't eat!"

Samson listened to their wild guesses and held in his laughter until he thought his sides would burst. "They'll never, never solve it," he chuckled.

Three days passed and still the Philistines had not solved the riddle. "We can't let Samson outwit us. We'd become the laughingstock of the village, not to mention what those Israelite farmers would say behind our backs."

"If we can't guess the answer, we'll get Samson's bride to find out what it is. After all, she's one of us."

"That won't be easy, since we're here to celebrate her wedding to Samson."

"She'll give in. I have a plan."

Samson's wife was sitting in the courtyard of her father's house when the young men approached her. "Find out the answer to Samson's riddle," they demanded. "Did you invite us to your wedding feast just so your Israelite groom could make fools of us? Help us win or else we'll burn your father's house to the ground!"

The young men left the bride with tears glistening on her cheeks. "How foolish of Samson to have started a contest in the middle of our wedding feast. He should have known my countrymen cannot abide to lose to an Israelite. Not even a battle of words! Surely Samson doesn't care about a silly riddle, not a man so big and strong."

The Timnite bride went in search of her husband. He was in the thick of a crowd of wedding guests. "You asked your attendants a riddle, but you haven't

told me the answer, dear Samson. Don't you trust me?"

"Of course I trust you, my love. But this is my own secret."

"Then tell me. Please! I want to share your secret."

Samson laughed and popped another fig cake into his mouth. "I haven't even told my parents, why should I tell you?"

Day after day, as the festivities continued, Samson's wife pleaded with her new husband. "You don't love me at all," she wept. "If you really loved me, you would tell me the answer to your riddle."

Finally Samson could stand the strain no longer. "Of course I love you." He tried hard not to lose his temper. "To prove it, I'll share my secret with you. One day, on the way to Timnah, I killed a ferocious lion with my bare hands," he boasted. "When I returned some time later to see what had happened to its body, there were bees in it—and handfuls of thick honey!"

"Now I see!" said his bride. "The strong eater is the lion, and the something sweet is the honey. What a strong husband I have and what a clever riddle."

A few hours later Samson encountered the young men. "Your time is up. It's not a sheep, not a goat. Time to pay up."

At first the Philistines pretended to be puzzled. Then they chanted in one voice,

> *"What is sweeter than honey,*
> *What is stronger than a lion?"*

Samson couldn't believe his ears. "Impossible," he shouted. "You could never have solved the riddle alone. You got the answer from my wife."

In a rage he left the wedding party and set off toward the Philistine city of Ashkelon. When he came upon thirty young men wearing fine linen garments, he tore their clothes off their backs. Then he hurried back to Timnah and presented the garments to the men who had tricked him. Still seething with rage, he returned to his father's house in the Danite settlement, saying not a word to anyone. Not even his wife.

It was the time of the wheat harvest. Samson's anger had finally cooled. He decided to return to his father-in-law's house to see his wife. "I'll let bygones be bygones and take her and her father a fine present." He strolled through the ripe grain fields thinking of his bride.

"I am sorry, Samson, but after you left, I assumed you didn't want my daughter for your wife." The old man looked up into the face of his son-in-law, who towered above him. He smiled meekly. "Maybe you'd like her younger sister to become your wife instead. She's much prettier."

"You Philistines will be sorry you tangled with me," growled Samson, more for the benefit of the Philistines standing nearby than for his apologetic father-in-law. "I'll really pay you back this time."

Off he stormed through the Philistine grain fields. A mean prank to play on the Philistines was taking

shape in his mind. He made his way through sheaves that gleamed in the summer sun. Wheat was stacked in neat piles; the harvest had just begun.

Crossing into the rocky open countryside, Samson got to work. In a short time he had rounded up three hundred foxes. "Not so difficult for a strong and clever fellow like me," Samson snarled and looked out at the Philistine fields below him.

Suddenly one hundred and fifty pairs of foxes with torches tied to their tails were racing through the neatly stacked sheaves of wheat and grain.

From their houses the Philistines saw smoke rising from the fields they had worked so hard to cultivate. Bundles of wheat burst into bonfires. The standing grain crackled. Within minutes the whole countryside was ablaze.

"No, not the vineyards too," the people cried when they realized that the spreading flames could not be quenched.

"And the olive orchards!"

From his lookout on the hillside Samson surveyed the destruction he had caused. With revenge in their hearts, the Philistines set out to find the one who had ruined their harvest.

"It's Samson, the son-in-law of the Timnite."

"Only Samson could be capable of such mischief."

"But why would he do such a thing?"

"Haven't you heard? His father-in-law married his daughter to the best man after Samson left the celebration."

The gossip spread as quickly as Samson's fire.

Filled with fury, the Philistines set fire to Samson's father-in-law's house. When Samson saw the remains of the house still smoking in the distance, rage burned within him. He rushed down the hillside and began grabbing Philistines, beating them up, and tossing them into the stubble of the grain fields.

Finally exhausted, his body bruised and his clothes torn, Samson limped off. "I'll go far away, where my enemies will never find me. I won't be the cause of trouble again."

He traveled alone until he reached the barren Judean hills. There in the cliffs of Etam he found a cave. "I'll hide out here until things cool down."

The Philistines searched for Samson throughout the territory occupied by the tribe of Dan. When they could not find him, they decided to mount an attack against the neighboring Judahites at Lehi. "When their families and fields are threatened, they'll give us Samson soon enough."

The Philistines had planned well. "Return to your own towns. We will capture Samson for you," agreed the Judahites. But as soon as the Philistines had withdrawn, the Judahites' attitude changed.

"Samson alone is stronger than ten of our soldiers."

"If the Philistines couldn't capture him, what chance do *we* have?"

"What chance do we have if we don't capture him?"

Slowly three contingents of Judahite soldiers crossed the rocky hillsides toward the cliffs at Etam. Outside his cave sat Samson.

"Samson! Come down and talk to us," one of the men shouted.

"Look at the trouble you've caused, leading the Philistines into our territory."

"I treated them as they treated me." Samson stood up, his back to the wall of solid rock.

"They rule over us. And we shall turn you over to them today. Our men are all over this hillside. You cannot escape."

"I will let you take me prisoner if you agree not to harm me yourselves."

"We'll bind you with cords and hand you over to the Philistines," they told him. "We have no wish to hurt you."

With new ropes the Judahites bound Samson and led him back to Lehi, where the Philistines were waiting. When they saw the mighty man's arms held fast to his sides with sturdy ropes, they cried out in triumph. As they ran toward their prisoner he snapped the ropes from his arms as easily as if he'd been bound with sewing thread.

A large bone lay on the ground near Samson. Fighting off the Philistines, he grabbed the bone and swung it over his head. Philistine helmets flew through the air. A few Philistines were hurled into the air. Samson swatted at his enemies as though they were insects.

In a short time the Philistines lay defeated. Samson composed a little rhyme to celebrate his victory.

> *"With the jawbone of a ruddy ass*
> *I piled them in a bloody mass."*

He was very thirsty after his battle, but only dusty hillsides and barren cliffs surrounded him. There was no water in sight. "O God," he cried out, "you have given your servant a great victory over the Philistines. But now I shall die of thirst. What will the Philistines think when they discover me dead? They'll say you were not powerful enough to save your servant."

Within moments Samson heard a loud crack behind him. Out of a hollow rock gushed cool water. Samson drank heartily. When he had refreshed himself, he set off toward his father's house in the camp of Dan.

Some time after he had tangled with the Philistines, Samson fell in love with a woman named Delilah. She lived in the valley of Sorek, where lush vineyards produced many varieties of succulent grapes. Since it was not far from the Danite camp, Samson visited Delilah often.

"You are as rich and mysterious as the wine from these grapes," Samson told Delilah while they sat in the arbor one afternoon. He reached up and pulled a cluster of grapes from the vine. Lazily, idling away the warm hours, he slipped the fruit into Delilah's mouth, one plump grape at a time.

One day the five leaders of the Philistines paid Delilah a visit. "If you can find out for us the secret of Samson's strength so that we may bind him and take him prisoner, each of us will reward you with eleven hundred pieces of silver."

That very day when Samson came to visit Delilah, she had set out dishes of his favorite food in the shade of the grape arbor. After offering him tastes from every plate, Delilah filled his glass again. "You are so strong, Samson. There is no man who can rival your strength. Not ten of the strongest Philistines are a match for you."

Samson nodded sleepily. After such a fine meal all he wanted to do was to lie down and rest in the shade, out of the hot midday sun. Delilah cracked a nut shell and handed Samson its meat. "Don't fall asleep before you answer me. There must be some way to tie you up so that you can't get away from me." She clasped him in her arms and laughed. "This isn't the answer. My arms won't even encircle your body."

"Not arms, Delilah, not even yours. But if someone bound me with supple bowstrings that had not yet dried out, I would grow weak. Then I'd be no stronger than any other man."

Soon Samson, heavy with wine, fell asleep. With seven supple bowstrings the Philistine leaders had brought her, Delilah bound Samson tightly while he slept. A few Philistines had hidden themselves nearby so that they could ambush Samson when Delilah gave them the signal.

"The Philistines are upon you, Samson!" cried Delilah. Immediately Samson jumped to his feet. He snapped the seven bowstrings as easily as though they'd been bits of yarn.

The next day Delilah again served Samson a splendid meal. She fed him all his favorite foods:

tiny olives and soft white cheese; juicy melon and cakes coated with thick amber honey. "Bowstrings you told me, and they were as useless as my poor little arms in holding you captive," Delilah chided him.

Samson held out his arms to Delilah. Veins crisscrossed his forearms like deep blue bands. "New ropes that have never been used, that would make me weak as any other man." As was his habit, he began to doze after his sumptuous meal. When she was certain he was deeply asleep, Delilah bound him with new ropes. Then she alerted the Philistines so that they could trap Samson when he awoke.

"The Philistines are upon you, Samson!"

No sooner had the words left her mouth than Samson snapped the ropes as though they were pieces of thread.

The next afternoon Delilah refused grapes from Samson's hands. "You fooled me again. All last night I wondered how someone could bind such a strong man. Not bowstrings, not ropes." She ran her fingers through Samson's long curly hair. "Please tell me the secret of your strength."

Samson held her hand and smiled shyly. "See how long and heavy my hair is, Delilah? If you weave the locks of my hair together with the flax on your loom, and pull the shuttle very tight, then I would become weak and be like other men."

While he slept, Delilah wove strands of Samson's long heavy hair into the flax of her loom. After pulling his hair as tightly as she could with the pin, she

cried out as she had twice before, "The Philistines are upon you, Samson!"

Samson woke and yanked his hair from the fabric she'd so carefully woven. Delilah stamped her foot as Samson strode out of the house, shaking bits of flax from his hair.

Day after day Delilah tried every way she knew to get Samson to reveal the secret of his strength. Other women might have given up, but Delilah was very determined. She desperately wanted the eleven hundred pieces of silver each of the Philistine lords had promised.

"You are the wittiest, most charming of all women. There is no other like you," Samson said one afternoon, his anger at Delilah's tricks forgotten.

"How can you say you love me when you won't share your secrets with me?" Delilah protested. "Three times I believed your stories about the secret of your strength."

"If it is so important to you—" He took her delicate hands in his.

"Oh, it is, Samson!" Delilah's face glowed with excitement. "Then I'll know you love me."

"I do love you, Delilah. To you I would reveal all my secrets. Before I was born, a messenger from the Lord appeared to my mother to tell her that I would be a Nazirite, a person dedicated to God's service. From the day of my birth until the day of my death. My long hair is a sign of my dedication to God. If my hair were to be cut, my strength would leave me, and I would become as weak as ordinary men."

Delilah knew that she had finally heard the truth. She sent word to the Philistine leaders. This time she was confident the reward they had promised would be hers.

The next afternoon after feeding Samson his favorite foods, Delilah coaxed him to rest his head on her lap. Very soon he was deeply asleep. Quickly she sheared his heavy hair.

"The Philistines are upon you, Samson," she whispered into his ear.

As he had each time before, Samson jumped to his feet, never believing he was in real danger. But the Philistines fell upon him and bound him with bronze chains. This time Samson could not escape. His enemies gouged out his eyes and brought him to Gaza, where they set him to work grinding at the prison-house mill. Hour after hour, day after day, dragging his heavy chains behind him, Samson turned the grindstone.

Time passed and Samson's hair began to grow back.

The Philistines were planning a great celebration for their victory over Samson. "We shall proclaim a great sacrifice to our god, Dagon. All the people will come. We must make it larger and more dramatic than any celebration in memory. For Dagon, our God, has given us our enemy Samson." The leaders' joy over their triumph did not lessen as the plans for the celebration grew more grand.

On the appointed day people began to arrive in Gaza at daybreak. One could barely move along the route. When the leaders paraded their prisoner through

the colonnaded streets, the people cheered and praised Dagon. "Glory to Dagon, who has ended the ravages of Samson. Never has one person brought such trouble to the Philistines."

The leaders, resplendent in their finest garments and jewelry, basked in the praise of the people. Leading Samson in his coarse shirt, they slowly made their way through the cheering crowds to the great temple of Dagon. The temple was so crowded, one could barely raise an arm to greet a friend. Three thousand men and women had squeezed themselves onto the roof of the temple so that they could watch the festivities.

"Bring Samson to the temple!" the people clamored. "Let him serve as amusement for us."

A young boy led Samson into the great temple of Dagon. The leaders made their prisoner stand between two of the massive center pillars that supported the temple. He could be seen by everyone in the huge crowd. The people on the roof looked down at Samson far below them.

Samson groped the air to either side of him. "Let me feel the pillars that hold up the temple so that I can lean against them," Samson asked the boy. The young Philistine felt sorry for the Israelite hero whose strength was reported to have been mightier than a hundred men. He took Samson's right hand and placed it against one stone pillar, and his left hand he rested on another.

"O Lord God, help me," Samson prayed. "Grant me strength this one last time. Let me show the Philis-

tines that you are the true God. Give me the strength to bring down this temple of Dagon upon the heads of those who worship him."

Samson pushed against the pillars with all his might. He groaned and strained until the muscles in his arms stood out like coils of new rope. A loud cracking and rumbling drowned out the sounds of laughter and triumph. Delight became dread as the foundations of the temple heaved and shook. Women and men were trampled underfoot as the crowd tried desperately to run from the doomed temple of Dagon.

A moment later the roof and all the people on it crashed down upon the crowd, crushing everyone.

Dagon's temple lay in ruins. Not one Philistine who had attended the victory celebration remained alive. Samson's prayer had been answered, and he died with his enemies. From that day on, Samson was honored as a hero in Israel, and people recalled that the power of the Lord God was the true secret of his strength.

Notes

Like Deborah, Samson is called a judge of Israel. But unlike Deborah he never leads Israelite troops into battle against their enemies or renders legal decisions. Given his unusual escapades, he is a very unlikely figure for a judge. But God's choice of an unlikely leader to further the divine plan is a common biblical motif.

The story of Samson, the strong man from the tribe of Dan, is set in the twelfth century B.C.E., when Israelites and Philistines were vying for control of the fertile plains of Palestine. It is easy to imagine how stories of Samson's adventures could have arisen as folktales. Stories of strength residing in the hair are common throughout folk literature, as are stories of a woman who betrays a man's secret to his enemies.

As an oppressed group forced to share the land with their enemies, the Danites must have reveled in telling how their hero got the better of the culturally and militarily superior Philistines.

The name Delilah is a pun on the Hebrew word for night, while Samson is related to the word for sun. Some translations have Delilah call a barber to cut Samson's hair. The Hebrew text indicates that Delilah shaves Samson, just as she bound him with ropes and wove his hair in her loom in her other attempts to capture him. Though Samson's death at the end gives the story a somber tone, it is not a tragedy. The victory of God, through Samson, over the Philistine grain god, Dagon, was cause for celebration in Israel.

SAUL AND THE
MEDIUM AT ENDOR

"Look at him, sitting alone, almost hidden in the dark crevices of the rocks. It's not right for a king to cower in the shadows, especially the night before an important battle," Rami said in a worried tone to his friend Yair.

King Saul, his sons, and his troops were preparing to battle the fearsome Philistine army, who were camped at Shunem, only a few miles away from the Israelite camp at Gilboa. As evening fell it became clear to Saul's loyal soldiers that the king of Israel had lost his taste for battle.

"Such an inspiring leader he was!" Yair smacked the ground. "I've been in his service since he delivered the people of Jabesh-gilead from defeat and humiliation by the Ammonites. What a warrior! No one could compare with him. But now he seems like a different man. I've never seen such fear in a leader."

"Yes, poor King Saul is a shadow of the great ruler

he used to be." Rami sighed. "When he began to rule over Israel, all the people believed he would defeat the Philistines. I've been with him since his youth, since the days before Israel had a king.

"He was hardly more than a boy when his father sent me with him to search for donkeys that had strayed from the herd. We'd wandered through the wilderness for three days. Our provisions were gone. Saul had lost heart and was ready to return to his father's house and admit failure. Then I suggested that we seek the advice of a prophet who lived nearby. Somehow I knew that he would be able to tell us precisely where those donkeys were to be found."

"Was that when the great Samuel anointed Saul king?" Yair asked.

"Yes," Rami replied. "But at the time I didn't know what had transpired. Samuel anointed Saul in secret, and Saul kept the news to himself for a long time. Even I, Saul's closest aide, did not know I was serving a king. He was so young; he didn't want to be king, you know."

Yair tossed a handful of sticks on the smoldering fire. "Then there was the time Goliath issued his challenge for an Israelite to meet him in hand-to-hand combat. Saul was frightened then—who wouldn't be at the sight of that terrible giant covered in armor! But even though he was afraid, King Saul was not pale and listless as he has been these last few days. I fear that he has lost hope."

"If only Samuel were still alive! He could advise Saul and encourage him, as he did in the past."

"Or if David were with us, perhaps he could deliver us, as he saved us from Goliath with a well-shot stone. If only Saul's jealous rage hadn't driven the young warrior into the countryside, to seek refuge among our enemies, the Philistines."

"You know, Yair, sometimes I think that God has forsaken Saul."

"If that is true, my friend, what is to become of Israel?" Yair tossed a rock into the ravine. "And what shall become of us?"

The two men gazed at the darkening sky, each lost in his own thoughts. Then Yair continued in a softer tone. "The Philistine troops have already assembled across the ridge at Shunem. Their army outnumbers ours by hundreds of men and arms. Who will save us now?" he called to the great silent sky.

"Hush. Here comes the king!"

Slowly, as though each step cost him dearly, King Saul approached his men. "Yair and Rami, my most valued servants, I need your help."

"We are here to serve you, my lord," they said together.

The king ran his hand over his weary face. "Day after day I have waited for the guidance of the Lord. I have listened, but God has sent me no word or sign.

"To show the whole kingdom my loyalty is solely to God, I drove all the wizards and soothsayers and mediums out of the land of Israel. And now I myself am in need of their talents. Is there a woman anywhere in my kingdom who could conjure up the spirit of someone dead?"

The two servants exchanged fearful glances. Neither spoke.

The king had a glazed look, as if seeing something beyond them. "There must be one," he whispered sadly. "One through whom I might hear again the voice—"

"Yes, my lord, there is a medium at Endor," Rami interrupted. "A wise woman an hour's journey from here, no more." His voice quavered.

The king gained fresh energy from this news. "We must consult her at once."

"Not now, surely, my lord," Yair protested. "You have not eaten a morsel of food all day. You must take some food, refresh yourself. Early in the morning, as soon as it is light and we have had some sleep, we will make the journey."

"We shall go immediately, under cover of darkness," the king said with royal firmness. "Find me something to wear as a disguise. The woman must not recognize me. If we are clever, she will not realize that I am the king."

Rami searched the tents of some of the king's officers while Yair rummaged about in his own baggage. Disguising the king was not a simple task. Saul was a large man, towering head and shoulders above most people. Finally his aides managed to find a suitable tunic of rough cloth and a long gray hooded robe for King Saul.

Sitting near the fire, as though in a dream, the king drew a crude map on the ground with a pointed stick. "We shall circle around the rear of the Philistine

camp. We need not worry if we move with caution. Sleeping Philistine soldiers will be more disturbed by the snores of their companions than by our few footfalls."

Yair and Rami were heartened by the decisive tone in Saul's voice. Wrapping cloaks around them against the cool night air, they followed their king down the hillside, away from the Israelite camp.

By the time they reached the house of the medium at Endor, it was pitch dark. There was no moon that night, and not a star glimmered in the sky. Rami rapped several times upon the door.

"Knock louder," said Yair. Just then someone opened the door a crack. A slight woman, her hair disheveled and a frayed garment thrown over her shoulders, peered at them.

Saul didn't wait for her to speak. "Can you conjure up for me someone's spirit?"

The woman stared at the three men, her eyes wide with alarm. Her face was kind, but she frowned as she leaned toward them, whispering in a confidential manner. "Everyone knows that King Saul has forbidden such things. He has driven the wizards and mediums out of the land. Believe me, my lords, you have been misinformed. I do not conjure spirits. I live here alone and sell the milk from my few goats." She hid her face behind the door. "The king would have a person put to death for conjuring a spirit."

"I swear to you," called Saul in an authoritative voice, "you will not be punished if you can do this thing."

The woman opened the door again and considered the three men for a moment. Then she opened the door wide so they could enter the room. Saul sat at a small table where a candle stub still burned. At a sign from the king, Yair and Rami sat a few feet away on a wooden couch and watched the eerie shadows cast by the candles on the opposite wall.

"Whose spirit do you want to consult?" The woman's voice was low and reassuring. Clearly the world of spirits did not frighten her.

"Samuel," the king replied after a moment's hesitation. He clasped and unclasped his hands. "Call the prophet Samuel for me."

The woman's eyelids closed. For several moments she remained still. Then her lips moved, but no sound came from her. She opened her eyes and seemed to search the dark. A wisp of smoke twisted in the light of the candle.

Suddenly the woman screamed. Yair leapt from the couch.

"You are King Saul!" she cried. "Why have you deceived me?"

"There is no reason to fear." He leaned forward, speaking urgently. "What do you see?"

"I see a spirit rising up from the underworld. Twisting and turning, it comes unwillingly."

"What manner of spirit comes?" Saul shivered, his hands clenched with fear.

"An old man is appearing." She squinted into the darkness. "He wears his flowing robe."

Rami and Yair waited with trembling hearts. The

room had turned dank and cold; their cloaks felt damp to the touch. Neither dared utter a sound. They could not see the king's face. Saul moaned and rose from his seat. Eyes squinted against the stunning sight before him, he bowed to the ground. They were in the presence of the ghost of Samuel.

The voice that broke the silence thundered through the small room.

"Why have you disturbed me by calling me up from the realm of the dead?"

Saul's voice cracked. "I needed to hear your voice. I am so alone. Prophets have given me no oracle. Dreams do not inform me of things to come. The Philistines are now camped a few miles from here. Tomorrow they will wage war against me, and God has forsaken me. Day after day I wait, but the Lord sends me no guidance. O Samuel! Tell me what to do. Guide my hand one more time in battle."

"If God has forsaken you, what do you think I can do?" Death had not dulled Samuel's sharp tongue. "You disobeyed God. You didn't carry out the command to destroy every Amalekite and all their possessions. I warned you that day when King Agag remained alive, and you and the people spared the best of the Amalekites' sheep and cattle, that God would give the kingdom of Israel to another. Now that time has come. David, your rival, will be king over Israel. And as for you, tomorrow you and your sons will join me in death, for God will allow the Philistines a great victory over Israel."

King Saul fell full length onto the cold dirt floor

and lay still as a piece of wood. A chill wind swept through the room, snuffing the candles. Only the woman seemed at ease. After she had relit the candles, the room held no trace of the prophet Samuel. But his words were burned into the memories of all who had heard them.

The woman turned to the two soldiers. "The king must rest for a while. All his strength has left his limbs." The king's body began to shake. "Has he been fasting in preparation for the battle?" the woman asked Rami and Yair.

They hurried forward to help their king. "He has eaten nothing all day. He refused all our offers of food. The only thing on his mind has been to find a way to consult the ghost of Samuel. Ever since he became king, he has needed Samuel when he has lost heart."

The wise woman leaned over the man crumpled on the floor. She touched his shoulder very gently and spoke softly, to comfort him. "I have obeyed you, calling the prophet Samuel away from his rest. At the risk of my life, I did as you asked. Now you must do as I ask. Let me prepare you a simple meal. Without nourishment, you will not be able to return to your camp this night."

"I cannot eat," he murmured into the folds of his robe. He made no attempt to rise from the floor.

Yair and Rami added their pleas to that of the woman. Finally the king allowed himself to be helped from the floor. He settled his body heavily onto the

couch where Yair and Rami had been sitting and stared dully at the wall.

The woman lit a fresh candle and set about her work. She prepared a fatted calf and took flour and kneaded it and baked flat cakes of bread. She set the steaming meal before Saul and his soldiers. They ate the hot food as quickly as she had prepared it.

Before the day dawned, Saul knew the time had come to return to the troops. Reluctantly they got up from the table and left the safety of the woman's house. In a few hours the battle would begin.

"It is a new day, my lord," the woman said as she bid King Saul and his men farewell.

Notes

Our story comes from the first book of Samuel, chapter 28. One of the Bible's great merits is its honesty about the hardships of life, and we have included this story to show that not all Bible stories end "happily ever after." Saul was Israel's first king. He was rejected by God for failing to destroy in battle all the Amalekites and their possessions. This is the incident to which Samuel refers in the story. In the battle against the Philistines that follows this scene, Israel is defeated, three of Saul's sons are slain, and Saul takes his own life by falling upon his spear. Saul's death opens the way for David to become king.

Rites involving consultation of the dead were strictly forbidden by biblical legislation but apparently occasionally practiced. This scene is unique in the Bible, for not only

does Saul consult a medium, but the woman is shown to have the power to conjure up Samuel's ghost. The circumstances of the appearance of the shade or ghost of Samuel are mysterious. Samuel, for example, appears to speak directly to Saul and not through the medium. Whether Saul's servants saw and heard the apparition is not clear.

DAVID—FROM
OUTCAST TO KING

◊◊ "The rumors are true. King Saul and his army have pursued us into the wilderness of Ziph." The news brought by David's spies spread quickly among his small band of followers. "They are encamped on the hill of Hachilah, close to the road. There must be three contingents of them."

"They do not know we're such a short distance from their camp." Ahimelech the Hittite put his hand on David's shoulder and let out a sigh of relief. "Our six hundred troops are no match for Saul's army. Early in the morning, before the sun rises, we can break camp and escape from them, as we have before."

"Not this time, Ahimelech," replied David. He squinted into the distance in the direction of Saul's camp. "Who will go down with me into the camp to Saul?"

"You can't be serious, my lord!" Ahimelech sprang forward in front of David. "It's the opportunity Saul

has been looking for; you'd be playing right into his hands."

"I'll go with you!" Abishai, one of the three sons of David's sister, rushed to David's side.

"Then let us leave camp quickly under cover of darkness."

As they made their way over the rugged terrain toward Saul's camp, Abishai spoke in hushed tones. "I'm glad we're not running from Saul again. You're a great warrior and the people of Israel love you. But ever since Saul decided that you pose a threat to his kingship, he thinks only of eliminating you. It's time you faced him down. This time we must fight!"

"Enough, Abishai! Even though Saul seeks my life, he's still God's anointed king over Israel and I am his subject. Be quiet now; there's the camp ahead."

The two men clung to the shadows as they skirted Saul's camp. Everything was as still as death.

The thick silence of the night was surprising. An army on the march sleeps with one eye open. But a deep sleep had fallen upon every man, from the king to his youngest foot soldier. Even the sentinels on guard duty were slumped over at their posts, their heads drooped over their weapons. Their few horses snorted in their sleep. Nearby, two field mice slept beside the leather harnesses they had been gnawing.

"There is Saul." David nodded toward a group of sleeping soldiers in the center of the camp. "Over there, surrounded by his guards, with Abner his general sleeping next to him."

David and Abishai walked stealthily to where the

king lay. Saul breathed heavily as if troubled by unquiet dreams. His spear was stuck in the ground next to his head.

"This is unnatural—standing over an enemy like this." Abishai made no effort to lower his voice as he looked down at the defenseless king. "God has caused this sleep like death to fall upon Saul and his soldiers. God has given your enemy into your hand. Let me pin the king to the ground with one stroke of his spear." The young warrior leaned over the sleeping monarch. "I won't have to strike him twice."

"Abishai, don't harm him!" David placed a restraining arm upon his nephew's shoulder. "Who dares put forth his hand against the Lord's anointed brings bloodguilt upon himself. No, King Saul will die in God's good time. Maybe he will be killed in some battle. But it is not for us to take his life. I will not shed the blood of the Lord's anointed. We'll take the spear beside his head, and the jar of water next to it, and return to our camp."

David yanked the spear out of the ground next to Saul's head. Then he grabbed the water jar, and he and Abishai strolled out of the camp unnoticed. Not one soldier had stirred in his sleep.

Day was breaking as David and Abishai crossed over to the top of a mountain overlooking Saul's camp. The steep and treacherous mountainside fell sharply, forming a deep valley that separated the two men from Saul's forces.

"Abner," David yelled at the top of his voice. "Abner, son of Ner, general of Saul's army, answer me, Abner."

Abner shook the sleep from his limbs and bolted to his feet. "Who is it who calls the king?" He looked around frantically, finally catching sight of a man on the mountain. The early morning sun was rising behind him.

"You are not worthy to be the general of an army of mice, Abner. Were you too tired to keep watch over your precious king during the night?"

"I never closed my eyes all night," Abner shouted back, his eyes scanning the hillside to see who dared taunt the king's general.

David laughed mockingly. "Then someone slipped into your camp while your eyes were wide open. He might have killed the king, while you and your brave soldiers slept as soundly as infants. With your eyes open."

"Nonsense. My king is safe," shouted Abner, reaching for his sword.

"Where is the king's spear and the jar of water that was at his head?"

Abner searched the ground where Saul lay. "Wake up, you lice!" Abner kicked at several of his soldiers.

"Too late now, Abner!" David's laughter rang down the mountainside.

Saul rose groggily to his feet and stood beside Abner. "Is that your voice, David?"

"Yes, my king. Why is my king pursuing such a loyal servant as I? What have I done that you seek my life like one who hunts a partridge in the mountains? If God has caused you to be angry at me, may God accept an offering. But if other people's talk has

turned you against me, then they have wronged me and caused me to be driven away. I mean you no harm. The king of Israel has amassed his army to chase a flea!"

Saul looked up at David standing on the rocky ledge. "I have wronged you, David," the king said, never taking his eyes from the young man he had once placed in command of his army. "I see now that my life was precious in your eyes."

All of Saul's troops were now awake and surrounding their king. With Abishai behind him, David stepped forward into the morning sunlight. Shouting, he brandished Saul's spear over his head. "Send one of your soldiers to collect your weapon. The Lord gave you into my hand today, but I would not lift my hand against the Lord's anointed. As your life was precious in my sight, so may my life be precious in the sight of the Lord."

"I and my troops will pursue you no longer," Saul called loudly. "I leave you with my blessing, David. I know you will succeed in all that you do."

"They're breaking camp," said Abishai later. "The king is as good as his word." He turned to David in astonishment. "We won't have to hide in the hills from King Saul any longer."

David shrugged his shoulders. "If only it were true. But I know that Saul won't stop until he's convinced I'm no longer a threat to his throne. We shall have to leave his territory. We have no choice but to seek refuge outside the borders of Israel, among Saul's enemies, the Philistines."

When they had packed their household goods, David and the six hundred men with him and their families prepared to set out for the Philistine city-state of Gath. David had decided they would enter the service of Achish, its king.

"We must be careful," David warned his followers, who were jubilant because they no longer had to fear Saul. "If we are to be safe in Gath, we must convince Achish of our loyalty. Of course our fellow Israelites in the territory of Judah must understand that we are not traitors."

Ahimelech tightened the girth on one of the donkeys. "How will we make Achish and his generals believe white is black? Who would imagine that David, son of Jesse, could be disloyal to his own people?"

Abishai moved closer to David. The flush of excitement gleamed on his eager young face. "We could surround Achish's army on the first moonless night. If we behead his leaders, we shall convince these Philistines of our might. Our swords will proclaim our loyalty to our people."

"You and your brothers are a bloodthirsty lot!" His uncle slapped him playfully. "We have neither the troops nor the weapons to attack and win. I want my men alive. If Achish believes we are loyal, we will live long enough to do the will of God."

David left his men and walked off a short distance, away from the hustle and bustle of the final preparations for the journey. Sitting on a hilltop, he looked down at the valley below. Since the day that Samuel

had secretly anointed him so long ago, he had known that someday God intended him to become king. He had a feeling that the time of his final triumph was drawing near. As God's intended king over Israel, no man's sword could stop him.

He returned to his men and spoke with great calm and authority. "We shall make raids against other peoples who dwell in the desert, and bring the spoil to Achish. But we'll tell him the great booty comes from victory over Judahites in the Negeb. If we kill all the people in each settlement, none will remain to bear witness against us."

"It is indeed a plan that will insure our safety," agreed Ahimelech.

Just as David had predicted, Achish accepted David as his vassal. He gave David the town of Ziklag, and David and his followers lived there among the Philistines for more than a year. When reports that David had fled to Gath reached Saul, he sought David no more.

As he had planned, David sent raiding parties to pillage the surrounding countryside, killing all the people and rounding up their sheep, oxen, donkeys, and camels. Achish grew wealthier from David's successful raids. The hillsides were dotted with the increased flocks and herds that David brought as proof of his loyalty to the king of Gath. Achish trusted David as much as his own Philistine warriors.

"And where did you raid today?" Achish asked, surveying with pleasure the piles of garments and weapons that David presented to him.

"Why, the Judahites of the Negeb!" David responded solemnly. "They are no match for David, the vassal of Achish."

In the spring of the year, when armies prepare to go to war, the Philistines mustered their forces at Aphek. Their plan was to march to Shunem to do battle with Saul's troops, who were encamped at Gilboa. Thousands of Philistine soldiers, heavily armed and anxious for battle, took their places in their military units.

Abishai waved his sword in the air. Battle was in his blood. But Ahimelech the Hittite approached David with misgivings. "How can my lord fight the people from whom he sprang? What will become of us when we are forced to draw swords against our brothers, the men of King Saul?"

"Do not worry. We will take our place with the troops of Achish, but there is much time before the battle," replied David. He smiled and would say no more.

Contingent after contingent of Philistine soldiers passed for review before their generals. David and his men brought up the rear with Achish and his forces.

"Why are these Hebrews marching with our men?" The Philistine generals motioned for Achish to fall out of the line of march.

"That warrior is David, my valued servant." Achish stood straight at attention. "He has served me well, for more than a year, ever since he deserted King Saul of Israel. I have the herds and flocks he pillaged from his own people to prove his loyalty."

"Are you a fool?" The commander bit off his words. "He can't go to war with us against Israel! Haven't you considered that in the heat of battle he might turn against us? What better way for him to reconcile himself with his former king than with the heads of these men here?"

Another of the generals gestured toward the group of Israelite soldiers grouped together at the back of Achish's contingent. "Have you forgotten what the women of Israel sang at their celebrations?

> 'Saul has slain his thousands,
> And David his ten thousands.' "

Achish opened his mouth to speak, but one glance at the angry faces of the generals changed his mind. "I shall send the man back to his camp at Ziklag."

With a heavy heart Achish returned to his place at the head of his troops and sent for his Israelite vassal. David's contingent of soldiers gathered behind him. "We are ready for battle. We are prepared to fight for our king." David saluted Achish.

The king of Gath cleared his throat. "You have been a good and faithful vassal while you have dwelt in my territory. I would gladly have you and your band march into battle at my side. But the Philistine generals insist that you return to Ziklag."

"But why?" David sounded affronted. "Have I committed a disloyal act since I entered your service? Why can't I go into battle to fight against the enemies of my king?"

"To me you're as blameless as an angel of God. But

the generals do not trust weapons in the hands of a man from Israel. You and your followers are to leave as soon as it is light."

"If that is my lord Achish's will." David bowed low and returned to his men.

The next day David and his followers set out for the land of the Philistines. On the third day, they saw smoke rising from their settlement at Ziklag in the distance.

"The whole city has been burned to the ground! Our families and homes have been destroyed!" Some of the men broke rank and raced toward the smoldering remains. Others sat on the ground and wept.

"Only the Amalekites could have done such a vile thing. While we were marching with Achish, they attacked our settlement."

"The city has been destroyed, but no sign of life remains. They have taken our wives and children captive. They have rounded up our livestock and stolen all our gold and silver."

The men spoke out angrily against David. "We should never have left our families undefended. How could we have agreed to your foolish plan to march with the Philistines?" Surveying the ruins all around them, the soldiers taunted their leader.

David looked nervously into the faces of his fearsome troops. "Let us consult God to see what we must do. Send Abiathar the priest to me."

Two of the men ran off to find Abiathar and bring him before David.

"What is God's will, Abiathar? Shall we pursue the

band of robbers who destroyed our city and captured our wives and children? Will we be able to overtake them?"

"God instructs us to pursue them and has promised we shall overtake them and rescue everything they took from us."

"Then we have no time to waste."

David and all six hundred of his followers set out immediately into the desert after the Amalekites. After they had been traveling for several hours, they reached the brook Bezor.

"We cannot go any farther," some of the men complained. "We have had little rest since we left Aphek. Everyone is exhausted from traveling so far in the heat of the day."

"Those who cannot continue will stay here and guard the equipment," said David. "The rest of us will cross the brook after the Amalekites."

While two hundred men stayed behind, four hundred went with David. As they continued their pursuit, they came across an Egyptian lying on the ground, exposed to the merciless sun. He was barely alive. David's men gave him some water to revive him. When he had regained consciousness, they offered him a piece of fig cake and two clusters of raisins. Soon the man was able to sit up and speak.

"Who are you and how did you get here?" David asked.

"I am an Egyptian. The servant of an Amalekite. We were returning from raids against the territory

of Judah and against Ziklag of the Philistines. My master left me here, since I was too ill to travel."

"Will you lead us to this band of Amalekites?"

"Will you promise not to kill me or to send me back to my master?"

"I promise." With the Egyptian leading them, David and his men set out after those who had destroyed their homes.

The clamor from the Amalekite camp was deafening. The soldiers were feasting and dancing in celebration of the enormous booty they had taken in their raids. David and his men, their spears at the ready, rushed against them, catching them completely off guard. As their companions fell beside them, Amalekite soldiers rushed here and there desperately searching for their weapons. Groggy from celebration, they were no match for David's forces. Only four hundred Amalekites managed to flee into the desert on camels.

In the stillness of the deserted Amalekite encampment David's soldiers joyfully reunited with their families. Children clung to their fathers. Wives told the terrors of the past days.

"We must give praise to God that our wives and children are all safe," David said when his followers had grown quiet again. He turned to the young boys leaning against their fathers' knees. "Remember, when you grow old enough to fight in the king's army, the speed of our own attack today, which scattered those Amalekite bandits like stones in the desert hills," boasted David. "Our flocks and our herds and all our

possessions—everything has been delivered into our hands this day!"

Once more a hero in the eyes of his men, David and his followers returned to Ziklag to await news of the battle between the Philistines and King Saul.

Three days after their return to Ziklag, a man from Saul's camp came to David's makeshift headquarters. His clothes were torn and he had smeared dirt upon his head like a man in mourning. He was brought immediately before David.

David rose from his stool and stared at the man's gaunt face. "From where have you come?"

"I have escaped from the camp of Israel." The man's voice shook with urgency.

"From the camp of Israel? From Saul?" David fired questions at the man. "How did it go? What happened in the battle?"

The man was still greatly agitated. "Many of Saul's soldiers have been slaughtered in battle. The rest have fled, leaving their land to the Philistines. Saul and his son Jonathan are also dead."

"How do you know that Saul and Jonathan are dead?"

"I was there, on Mount Gilboa, where the most violent fighting took place. By chance I happened upon King Saul. He was wounded so badly that I knew at a glance he could not live. The king called to me and begged me to take his life so that his agony would be at an end. The Philistine chariots and horsemen were closing in, and since I knew there was no hope for him, I did as he asked."

David sat down on his stool and gripped its legs. He looked intently at the young man, who continued his report. "Here are his crown and insignia. I have brought them to you, for they should now be yours."

David reached out and took the crown and bracelet. "Where are you from, young man?"

"I am an Amalekite whose family lives in Israel."

On hearing that the young man belonged to the same people who had raided Ziklag only a few days earlier, David could contain his anger no longer. "How is it that you were not afraid to put forth your hand against the Lord's anointed? Guards, seize him!"

David turned to the Amalekite, who did not even struggle against the young men surrounding him. "Your blood is upon your head, for you testified against yourself when you boasted of slaying the Lord's anointed!" Full of cold rage, David gave the order. "Put him to death!"

David called his people together. "Today we must mourn the deaths of all the valiant Israelites who perished in battle against the Philistines. And we shall mourn for Saul also. Even though he pursued us, he was still our king, and he died protecting our country from our enemies."

The people joined with David and tore their clothes and fasted and wept, as was the custom. Late into the evening they grieved over their fallen countrymen.

Grieving publicly over Saul and Jonathan, David composed a beautiful elegy for the fallen monarch and his son:

"Your glory, O Israel, is slain upon the mountains.
How are the mighty fallen!"

After Saul's death, David and his followers left the Philistine city of Ziklag and returned to David's homeland of Judah, where David was crowned king. Some years later, David was made king over the northern tribes. David was thirty years old when he began to rule, and he reigned forty years. At Hebron he reigned over Judah seven years and six months. At Jerusalem he reigned over all Israel and Judah thirty-three years.

Notes

Our story comes from 1 Samuel 26 through 2 Samuel 1 and chronicles David's adventures from a time after he left Saul's service up to his kingship. David's anointing as Israel's future king was secret, and Saul remained king over Israel until his death on Mount Gilboa. David was a popular warrior in Saul's army, and Saul very early realized that the young hero was a threat to his kingship. Thus on numerous occasions he sought to kill David and finally drove him out of Israelite territory.

David became the leader of a kind of renegade band made up of malcontents and social outcasts. Like David they were fugitives who for social or political reasons were forced to live in the hills and raid nearby villages to survive.

David's rise to kingship over Israel occurs without any serious obstacles. Whether David is genuine in his protestations of loyalty to Saul or just biding his time is open to

question. We have tried to maintain some of the ambiguity surrounding David's motivations. For example, David tells Achish that he is anxious to fight on behalf of his king. Achish assumes David is speaking of him, but David could be referring to Saul.

There are two accounts of Saul's death. In the one preserved in 1 Samuel 31, Saul commits suicide by falling on his own sword. The Amalekite who tells David another version of Saul's death (2 Samuel 1) may be lying in hopes of gaining a reward from David, since now that Saul is dead, the way is cleared for David's succession to the throne.

THE WISDOM
OF SOLOMON

When King David
was nearing the end of his life, he appointed his
son Solomon to rule in his place. So it was that
Solomon, the son of David and Bathsheba, was
anointed king over Israel and Judah by Zadok the
priest and Nathan the prophet. The priests and the
people prayed that Solomon would be an even greater
king than David. "Long live King Solomon," they
cried, playing on pipes and rejoicing with such great
fervor that the earth was split by their noise. "May
the Lord God make the name of Solomon even greater
than his father's."

Solomon kept his promise to King David to love
God and to follow God's laws. Before the temple had
been built in Jerusalem, Solomon went to Gibeon to
worship and sacrifice to the Lord. There the Lord
God appeared to him in a dream one night. "Ask of
me whatever you want, and I shall give it to you."

Solomon dreamed of silver as common as stone in Jerusalem; he thought of a port filled with a fleet of ships bearing his royal insignia. In his dream he saw a great ivory throne decorated with finest gold. The throne had six steps with a lion guarding both ends of each step, and at the back was a calf's head. At each armrest a fierce lion stood poised to pounce.

Solomon sought to answer the Lord God. "My father kept his heart only for you, O Lord. He brought the ark of the covenant to Jerusalem, and now, following in the ways of my father, my dearest wish is to build a great and glorious house in Jerusalem in which the ark may rest forever. You have made me king over your great people, but what do I, a young man, know of justice and being a good ruler? So what I ask of you is wisdom and understanding so that I may govern your people and do you honor."

God was greatly pleased with Solomon's request. "Because you did not ask for a long life for yourself or for enormous wealth or kingly power, a fleet of ships or goblets of gold, because you did not ask for your enemies to be handed over to you, but instead you asked for a heart that could dispense fair judgment to my people, I shall grant your wish. You shall possess the wisest mind, able to render difficult decisions and to solve the most confounding problems. You will understand what no one has been able to discern before you. And there shall never be another person on earth with wisdom equal to yours. Also it pleases me to give you all the things you did not request. You will be richer than any other ruler and

you shall have as much honor as wealth, so that no one can compare with you all the days of your life. And if you keep my commandments, then you shall have a long, prosperous life."

When Solomon awoke and remembered all that the Lord had said to him in his dream, the king returned to Jerusalem, stood before the ark of the covenant, and offered prayers to God. Then he held a great feast of thanksgiving for all his court. The celebration lasted many days.

Not long afterward two harlots were brought into the king's chamber, each screaming insults to the other. In spite of the guards' efforts to silence the wrangling women, they continued to argue. One held an infant close to her, and the other woman held fast to her arm, never taking her eyes off the squirming child.

"Silence! You are in the presence of the king," commanded Solomon, clapping his hands sharply. His words echoed through the huge vaulted room like the cracks of a whip. The women were quiet for a moment, but the one clung to the child and the other continued to grasp her braceleted arm.

King Solomon observed that they were about the same age and they had dressed hastily. The hair of one woman was falling into her eyes. The second woman had stains on her robe. Clearly they were not women from his royal court.

The woman not holding the child released her grip on the other woman and stepped a few paces nearer to the king's great carved chair. "My lord, this woman

and I live in the same house. I gave birth to a healthy boy four days ago. Yesterday, when we were alone in the house, she gave birth to a boy child also. We were the only two in the house at the time."

The baby made a noise and the woman looked over to where it rested in the other woman's arms. The king tried not to look impatient with the laborious recounting of the story. These women with the pale baby were the tenth case he had heard that morning. "Then what happened?" he asked.

"While we slept, in the middle of the night, she must have rolled over on her baby and smothered him—"

"Liar! Filthy liar!" the second woman shouted, her face twisted in rage. The infant began to howl.

"Silence!" thundered the king. He turned to the first woman and motioned for her to continue her story. The baby kept up his persistent cries.

"She got out of bed in the middle of the night and crept over to where I was sleeping. She snatched my beautiful healthy baby from where he slept in my bed." She paused and looked over at the infant, who had turned red-faced from crying. "Then she placed the dead child in my arms in my bed. Early in the morning, when I arose to nurse my baby, I knew in an instant that the child wrapped in the blanket was not my child!" She covered her face with her hands and wept.

"No, my king, the living child is mine," the other woman insisted. She tried to quiet the infant, stroking his face and tiny fists. But his screams continued to fill the chamber.

The king gripped the arms of his chair. It was a very hot day and his viceroy had told him several more disputes awaited his decisions. Solomon observed the first woman, crying softly, and the second woman nuzzling the infant's cheek in an effort to soothe him.

"The dead child is hers. That child is mine!" the first woman cried. She seemed suddenly to realize that she was in the presence of the king and raked her hand through her long matted hair.

The second woman smiled at the king and spoke in a gentle voice. "Clearly the child belongs with me." She moved a few steps toward the men of the royal guard, holding the irritable child in front of her, as though asking for their confirmation.

The two women continued to quibble back and forth until the king could listen no longer. "Each one claims the baby is hers. You say your son is alive and hers is dead, and you say hers is dead and yours is alive." He turned to a guard. "Bring me a sword."

The king held the sword by its elegant bone handle. Its slender double-edged blade gleamed in a ray of sunlight. Sprays of light were reflected off the thick draperies at the window. The baby's gaze was fixed on the dancing rays of light. He was finally quiet. "My judgment is to divide the child in two. One half of the child shall go to one woman, one half to the other."

Upon hearing the words, the first woman rushed forward and knelt before the king. "Oh my lord, give

the living baby to her. But please, do not kill him. Please let him live."

But the second woman offered the baby to the king. "If that is what my lord has decided, I shall abide by your decision willingly. It shall be neither mine nor hers. Divide it."

Solomon twisted the great gold lion ring on his left hand. He studied the pattern of gold threads running through his robe. "Give the child to the first woman, and do not kill him. She is his mother."

When word of King Solomon's remarkable decision spread throughout the kingdom, the people were in great awe of their ruler. For they knew that only with the wisdom of God could anyone render justice as Solomon did.

God continued to give Solomon wisdom beyond measure. People said the king's knowledge spanned as many subjects as the grains of sand that lined the seashore. It was claimed that no one in the East or in the fabulous kingdom of Egypt was as wise as Solomon. He proclaimed three thousand proverbs and composed a thousand and five songs. He could speak about the trees, from the stately cedars of Lebanon to the small hyssop that seems to grow out of the rock itself. He explained the habits of beasts and birds and reptiles and fish and categorized each group according to its special characteristics. Leaders from all the peoples of the world came to Solomon's court to hear his wisdom and learn from him about everything under the sun.

Solomon held spellbound with all that he knew the

members of his court and the visitors who came from all the lands of the world. The day's light would fade into night, the candles would burn to stubs in the torches, and the king would still be spinning stories, enthralling his audience with descriptions of wild beasts, herds that had been seen by not one visitor seated at the king's table, plants that bloomed but once in ten years unseen in the wilderness.

Word of Solomon's wisdom and the enormous wealth of his kingdom and the opulence of his palace spread to distant kingdoms. The queen of Sheba, who ruled the arid land of Arabia, heard about Solomon and decided to visit the monarch, to test him with hard questions. Like Solomon, the queen was renowned for her knowledge and skills, and her subjects prospered.

It took many months for the queen of Sheba to prepare for her journey to visit the king of Israel and Judah. "This will be my most important alliance. Glittering jewels and words of wisdom will show the splendor of Sheba to one who has heard rumors of our greatness, and now will know the sparkle of our wit."

Everyone in the kingdom helped the queen prepare for her journey. Finally the day came to depart. From the walls of the queen's palace as far as the eye could see, caravans of camels began their trek across the desert.

"If he is truly as wise as they say he is, I shall present King Solomon with more spices than all the rulers who have visited him," the queen decided.

Some of her servants loaded the camels with cinnamon, calamus, nard, frankincense, saffron, myrrh, and aromatic oils of aloe and balsam. Others guarded great sacks filled with gold, pearls, silver, topaz, emeralds, and carnelian. Young women carried in sandalwood boxes the jewels that the queen wore: earrings of gold and sapphire; brooches of onyx; signet rings of amethyst; armlets and bracelets of copper, bronze, silver, and gold; coral and crystal pendants; and amber amulets and filigreed rings set with jasper and diamonds.

The queen's palanquin had posts of silver and a back of gold. Throughout the journey across the desert, sixty servants surrounded their ruler. Day after day she devised proverbs and riddles to stump King Solomon. "What is sweeter than honey and stronger than a lion?" she asked her courtiers. None guessed the answer. "It's love," the queen answered triumphantly.

"What four things on the earth are very small but very wise?" The queen's servants could not solve the riddle.

The queen waited for the moment when she might test the riddle on Solomon. Like the best of riddles, the answer once heard seemed simple. "No one thinks of ants as strong, yet they provide their own food in the summer; badgers have no might, yet they make their homes in the rocks; locusts have no ruler, yet they all march in rank; the common lizard no wider than my hand lives in the palaces of kings."

The people of Israel had never seen a caravan as long and splendid as the one approaching the city of

Jerusalem. For days the servants of the king and the servants of the queen of Sheba unloaded the camels.

Dazzled by the queen's beauty and the sharpness of her mind, King Solomon set about to honor his royal visitor with the most lavish banquet ever held in the kingdom of Israel and Judah.

The guests reclined on couches covered with gold and silver cloth, while servants offered them platters of grapes, figs, dates, and pomegranates. Court musicians played while the guests sipped wine from golden goblets. The queen of Sheba sat to the right of the king and amused him with riddles and wise sayings. "Like a jewel in a pig's snout, so is a handsome man without discretion."

"Another one, fair queen," pleaded the king.

"One who loves silver shall not be satisfied with silver. But as you have said yourself, O most wise Solomon, as money protects, so does wisdom. Wisdom lights up the face."

Before them the table was laden with mounds of goat cheese and butter molded into shapes of small animals and birds. Jars of wild honey stood next to great stacks of fig cakes. Hour after hour royal wine flowed.

Servants staggered under the weight of a gold platter holding a whole roasted gazelle. Following them, more servants brought steaming bowls of onions and lentils, beans and cucumbers. Solomon turned to his guests. "Eat your food in joy, drink your wine with a glad heart, since God has already approved what we do."

"You have been praised in all lands for your extravagant hospitality. But the food of your table surpasses that of all the rulers of the East," the queen of Sheba told her host.

"Even the rarest and sweetest wine does not do justice to the queen of Sheba." The king rose to toast his fair guest. "May wisdom be your constant companion wherever you go."

In her turn the queen rose to honor Solomon. "I shall give you gold to build a fleet of ships, spices to trade, and jewels to ornament your palace. But none of these things can compare with the wisdom you have shown to me. I shall leave with more than the simple gifts I brought."

"Wisdom has made us both rich beyond measure," the king assured her. "The words from your mouth have enriched many in this court; teach a just person and she will increase in knowledge."

The courtiers toasted the queen and applauded her.

The queen of Sheba took a sip from her goblet of wine. "I leave you with a riddle. Perhaps you will bring its answer if you will be kind enough to return my visit and honor our kingdom with your royal presence."

The king was delighted. "Another splendid riddle! May this one serve to end the meal, to honor our trade routes, to seal our friendship."

"Look over there, your majesty, alighting on that sconce! Two insects, flying at the same speed. Each has one pair of incandescent wings. Hear them buzz!" She waved her jeweled hand toward the insects flying

near the candle's flame. "How can one tell from such a distance which of these insects is a bee and which is not?"

King Solomon stared at the tiny shadows the two insects cast upon the wall. Then he arose and leaned over a cluster of bright blossoms in a silver bowl. Breaking off a stalk of lilies, he placed one in the hands of his guest. "The answer to your riddle is in your hand. The answer to your invitation is in the hands of God."

Notes

King Solomon was famous for his wisdom and his wealth. From his father David he inherited a kingdom that had been consolidated and expanded through military campaigns. Solomon's reign appears to have been a time of peace, security, and commercial expansion. Solomon is celebrated for his magnificent building projects, especially the temple in Jerusalem.

Our story represents only part of the biblical picture. There is evidence that Solomon was not an ideal king or a particularly wise ruler. To supply his lavish court, Solomon levied heavy taxes on his subjects. His massive building projects required prodigious labor, and the biblical text suggests that Solomon may have imposed forced labor on his own people, a cruel echo of their status as slaves in Egypt and a confirmation of the evils of kingship the prophet Samuel recites in 1 Samuel 8. Perhaps the clearest sign of political dissatisfaction with his reign is the fact that upon Solomon's death the kingdom split into two parts. The North-

ern tribes formed a separate kingdom and a descendant of Solomon retained the throne in the South.

The fanciful story of Solomon's judgment between the claims of two women to the same child and that of the visit of the queen of Sheba, located in southwest Arabia, are intended to illustrate Solomon's legendary wisdom and wealth. Besides the account in the Bible there are other legends about the queen of Sheba and King Solomon, including some that recount their marriage.

ELIJAH, THE
PROPHET OF GOD

Elijah, the prophet of God, went to Ahab, king of Israel, to warn him that the land would be troubled by a long drought. "In the name of the Lord God of Israel I proclaim to you that there shall be no rain, not even a drop of dew, except by the will of the Lord God."

The king was not particularly worried. There were many prophets in the land. Some said rain; some forecast drought. Queen Jezebel scorned Elijah and ignored his words of doom. "My prophets will call upon the Lord Baal-hadad to send us rain," she assured her husband.

Following the word of the Lord God, Elijah traveled east and camped at a brook on the far side of the Jordan River. God had promised Elijah that ravens would bring him bread and meat in the morning and in the evening. And so it happened. Elijah drank from the cool clear water of the brook. He splashed

water over his face and arms to refresh himself. Elijah wondered how long he would be able to rest in the shade by the brook. After a few days he noticed that the water was gradually drying up. There had been no rain, as the Lord God had declared. Soon the broad flat stones of the riverbed glistened in the sun. The ground cracked open and became like clay.

The word of God came again to Elijah, telling him to move on. This time he was to journey far to the north, beyond Israelite territory. "When you arrive at the town, a widow will feed you."

"That is how I'll know I'm there," Elijah said to himself and began walking. Morning and evening, there was not a cloud in the sky. Even if the king didn't believe his prophecy, Elijah knew God would not send rain until the right time.

As soon as he came to the gate of the city, Elijah saw a woman, her head bent over her chest, wearily gathering sticks.

"Would you bring me a small pitcher of water? I am very thirsty," he called to her. As she went to get it he called after her, "Could I please have a piece of bread also?"

Sadly she shook her head. "I have no bread. Only a handful of flour is left—and a few drops of oil. I was gathering sticks to make a fire. I shall bake a single flat bread for my son and me, and then I fear we shall die. For there is no grain, there is no money, and there is no rain cloud in the sky."

Seeing her grief, Elijah drew himself up to his full height. "You need not worry. The Lord God of Israel

has said that your jar of flour shall not be empty.
Bake me a small loaf of bread. There will be enough
for you and for your son."

"There is not enough for even one loaf." Dismayed,
she held up her jar with its few drops of oil.

"The oil shall be replenished too!"

And it was exactly as Elijah said. For many days
he and the woman and her son ate as much as they
needed to satisfy their hunger. It was just as God had
promised Elijah.

But after a while the woman's son grew ill. No
herbs or salves made the boy better. Finally his body
shuddered and he stopped breathing. For a moment
there was a terrible stillness in the room. Then the
boy's mother shrieked. Elijah hurried to her side.
Moaning, she cradled the lifeless child close to her.

"What do you have against me, man of God? Ever
since you came here, strange things have happened,"
she wailed. "Why have you come to my house, first to
save our lives with food and now to bring death to
my only son?"

"Let me take the boy." Elijah held the child in his
arms and carried him to the upper room where he
had been staying and laid him gently on the bed. The
boy did not move.

"O God, how could you strike this boy, the son of
the woman you sent me to? How could you do this to
me—your prophet?"

When he saw that the boy lay still as a stone, he
leaned over the small, lifeless body and cried aloud to
God. "Please, O Lord God, send breath back into him.

Please hear your prophet Elijah!" The boy's eyelids flickered. He opened his eyes and looked around, puzzled at being in the upper room. He stretched and took a deep breath.

Wrapping the boy in his cloak, Elijah went downstairs. The widow was rocking herself in a corner of the room, weeping softly.

"Look, your son lives. His eyes are open, and a healthy glow has returned to his face. He is full of life."

The mother held her child on her lap, smoothing his hair and kissing his cheek. Looking up at Elijah, she said, "I am sorry I doubted you. Now I know that you are a prophet of God. The words of God that you speak are true. The Lord God of Israel has returned my son to me."

The drought dragged on for three long years, bringing famine and desperate hardship to the people. The word of God came again to Elijah, telling him to return to King Ahab. So he left the widow and her son and journeyed south toward Israel.

Conditions were particularly severe in Samaria, where King Ahab and Queen Jezebel lived. King Ahab called Obadiah, the steward of his palace, to him. "All the springs and brooks are drying up. Even the cattle are dying of thirst. Search out the countryside to the north, perhaps we shall find enough grass to keep the horses and mules alive. I shall search the land to the south."

Obadiah set out to follow the king's orders. He

was an honorable man who loved God. When Queen Jezebel sought to wipe out all the prophets of the Lord God, Obadiah had hidden a hundred of them, fifty at a time, in caves outside the city walls and brought them food and water every day.

When he had been walking for a long time, and his own supply of water was quite low, Obadiah scanned the cloudless sky. There was no sign of rain. On the road, far ahead of him, he saw a man.

"I'll ask him if any grass remains over that far hill," Obadiah decided. "And save myself a hot dusty walk."

As the man approached, the sunlight fell upon his face. "Elijah!" cried Obadiah. "You have been away so long!" He bowed low to the prophet of God.

"Go and announce to the king that Elijah has returned. I bring word from the Lord God of Israel." Elijah fastened his cloak more tightly around him. "Hurry now!"

Obadiah shook his head and dug his foot in the dirt, stirring up a small cloud of dust along the roadside. "You have been away, so you do not know the situation here. The queen has determined to rid the kingdom of all the prophets of the Lord God, while the prophets of Baal and Asherah enjoy royal protection. Ahab has been searching through every settlement, to the farthest points in the kingdom, even to other nations. Everywhere the king's men ask for you. When Ahab receives word that you are not to be found in this or that town, he makes the people take their oath on it. Knowing these things, do you still want me to announce your presence to the king?"

"Hurry, Obadiah, go to Ahab and tell him that Elijah comes with the word of God."

"When he hears this message, he will surely kill me," Obadiah insisted. "You know I am loyal to the God of Israel. Haven't I hidden a hundred of God's prophets in the cliffside caves? Haven't I risked my safety bringing them food and water? Now you want me to tell the king to his face that Elijah is coming." He sat down in the dust and covered his face with his hands.

"The king is asking for Elijah, well, Elijah is asking for the king. He wants to see me; all right, then, Obadiah, tell him today he shall see the prophet of God."

Obadiah shook the dust from his cloak and set off down the road to search for King Ahab. "And when the wind carries you away, as it always seems to, and I say Elijah has come, and then Ahab is unable to find you —" Obadiah muttered and slowed his step, not relishing this announcement to the king.

As soon as King Ahab heard about Elijah's return, he hastened to meet the prophet. Confident of the king's arrival, Elijah waited in the road. The king's face twisted into an angry frown. "So you have returned, you troublemaker."

"It is you and not I who is the troublemaker," replied Elijah sarcastically. "You and those around you who have disregarded the commandments of the Lord God and chosen to follow the Baals."

"You dare to question the king?" Ahab shouted.

But Elijah held his ground. "Gather all the people together, and the four hundred prophets of the great

Baal," he growled with a sneer. "Meet me on Mount Carmel. And bring the four hundred and fifty prophets of Asherah, who receive their support from the queen."

The king did as Elijah asked. "Once and for all we shall silence this little man with his big words of doom," Ahab vowed. "He will make a fool of himself in front of all Israel. Then his words will prove to be as empty as the water troughs, and he shall trouble us no more."

The king sent for the prophets of Baal, who came to Mount Carmel surrounded by a crowd of followers. There was a feeling of excitement, as though it were a festival. Children ran after their parents, wondering at the sudden laughter among the prophets.

"What could Elijah have up his sleeve?" one of the Baal prophets asked.

"I left the palace without eating any of the delicacies the queen's cooks had just prepared, so whatever his plan, it had better be worth the trip," his friend replied.

"How could it be otherwise; all of us and one of him," another answered gleefully. "This is the day we quench the fire in Elijah's words."

Elijah strode through the crowd of Israelites, muttering to himself. The people bowed respectfully to him, but a moment later they honored the prophets of Baal equally. It was too much for Elijah to bear.

"You miserable cowards. How long are you going to divide your loyalties? If you believe in the Lord God of Israel, then you must give all your loyalty to

my God. If in your foolishness you put your faith in the Baals, then save no smile for me or my God."

Seeing Elijah's face contorted with anger, his long white hair standing up around his head, the people said nothing. The other prophets snickered. "Pay no attention to him. What sort of God has only one prophet? See how many there are of us."

Elijah tore at his cloak. "For once he has spoken the truth, this dog-faced, caper-nosed prophet of Baal. For I am the prophet of the true God and soon we shall all know where the power of God lies."

"With us!" shouted the four hundred prophets of Baal.

"With us too!" shouted the four hundred and fifty prophets of Asherah.

"Only with the Lord God of Israel," Elijah shouted alone.

Stunned by the clamor of the prophets, the people backed away and stood apart. Children clung to their parents' hands.

Elijah seemed to gain new energy from the silence of the crowd. "Have two bulls brought here. Since there are four hundred of them"—he gestured toward the mass of prophets across the way—"they can select their animal. I shall take the other. We shall each lay the wood upon the altar for the sacrifice, we shall prepare the bull, but we shall not light the fire under the wood."

"That's the silliest idea—" The prophets laughed, and the people with them.

"You call on the great Baal to light the fire for your

sacrifice and I shall call on the Lord God of Israel, and the God who answers with fire, that one is the true God."

"Yes, that is good. Well done, Elijah." The people murmured their approval.

Elijah clapped his hands. "You first. Prepare your sacrifice but do not light it. Then call on the great Baal to send you fire."

The prophets set to work and soon had prepared a great mound of dry sticks. They laid the bull on top of it and came together to call upon Baal.

> *"O Lord Baal, send us fire to ignite the wood,*
> *So the people may worship you as they should."*

Over and over they cried from morning until the sun was high in the sky, but the tinder remained cool and the breeze stirred not at all.

> *"O Baal, send us flame,*
> *We call upon your mighty name."*

The people whispered among themselves. Elijah laughed and snapped a twig in two. "Better stand back. When that pile of wood bursts into flame, it will make a mighty blaze. Mighty as Baal himself."

The prophets fell upon the ground and cried to Baal. They threw off their cloaks and they limped around the cold altar.

Elijah rested his hand on the highest mound of sticks. "Not too strong, this Baal. But maybe he's

taking a nap. Try calling louder, perhaps you can wake him! Or maybe he's thinking of more important matters, like the grape harvest, to have time for a mere four hundred prophets calling his name."

The prophets snatched up their cloaks and flung them at the sky.

> *"Baal, send us flame,*
> *We cry aloud in your mighty name."*

Elijah went toward the crowd. "You must be getting tired, waiting so many hours in the hot sun, waiting for fire that would feel even hotter than the sunlight on this mountain. Maybe Baal has gone off on a journey far from this mountain. What do you think of him now?"

The people whispered their shame. The prophets grabbed sticks from the cold pyre and flayed themselves, crying aloud to Baal. But no answer came; not a sound. Not even a spark appeared among the twigs upon the altar.

"Now if you'll all gather near me, I shall repair the altar of the Lord God of Israel. We shall use twelve stones, for the twelve tribes of Israel, and build up an altar to God." As he worked, Elijah continued to address the people. "No one shall destroy an altar to God again, not in the name of Baal, nor in the name of Asherah."

He dug a wide and deep trench around the altar. While he prepared the bull for the sacrifice he turned to the people standing closest to him. "Soak this wood with four pitchers of water."

They looked at each other in disbelief but did as he ordered. The prophets of Baal stayed close together near their own cold altar.

"Now pour four more pitchers. Be sure to soak it well." Some children hurried to help fill the pitchers.

"That's good. Now again, so that the water fills even the trenches."

"Wasting water in the midst of a drought," jeered one of Baal's prophets.

"The Lord God can send water, as the Lord can send fire," Elijah assured him, not pausing in his work.

Finally, when he saw that everything was ready, Elijah raised his arms. The crowd grew still. The prophets of Baal grew still. Elijah's voice rang out across the mountainside. "O Lord God of our ancestors, let it be known this day that you alone are God over Israel, and that I, Elijah, am your prophet, that I have done all that I have done and spoken all that I have spoken at your command. Answer me, O God, so that the people will know that you are God. You alone."

Suddenly a great fire fell from heaven and the wood burst into flame. The people backed away from its powerful heat. The wood crackled, the water sizzled, and instantly the trench was dry. When the people saw that the offering had been consumed and not so much as a twig remained on the ground at Elijah's feet, they knelt where they had stood and worshiped the Lord God of Israel, crying again and again, "The Lord alone is God."

At Elijah's command, the people fell upon the prophets of Baal, who had been defeated that day. When Elijah came down the mountain with the people of God, not a single prophet of Baal remained to scoff at the Lord God of Israel.

Ahab had been watching the contest with his courtiers. Elijah went up to the king, a smile of great satisfaction brightening his usually grim face. Surveying the scene around him, Ahab turned away from the prophet. Queen Jezebel would be furious when she heard what had befallen her prophets. "Haven't you caused enough trouble for one day?" The king called for his chariot.

"You haven't seen anything yet." The prophet circled around the king. "Go home, eat and drink. The famine will soon be over, for a great rainstorm is coming."

While Ahab was returning by way of Jezreel, Elijah climbed up to the top of Mount Carmel. He sat down on a large flat rock, clasped his knees to his chest, and rested his head on them. After a while he beckoned to the young man who attended him. "Go look out over the sea and tell me what you see."

The young man looked down at the vast blue sea far below him. He returned a moment later. "The water is calm and there is no cloud in the sky."

"Go back seven times." Elijah sat quietly, waiting.

Finally the young man came back, his face keen with excitement. "There is a cloud, a small puff of a cloud, about the size of your hand, Elijah, rising out of the sea."

Elijah was not at all surprised. "You'd better tell the king to prepare his chariot. If he doesn't leave

now, the road may be washed out and the wadis so full of water that a mud slide might block his path."

Quite soon the sky darkened. The king's chariot was still on its way down the valley toward Jezreel when the rain began to fall in torrents. The winds raged over Mount Carmel, knocking apart the deserted altars of Baal. Rain beat upon Elijah's upturned face. His cloak clung to his wet body. The wind carried the rain like a solid wall and flung it against the high peaks. The altars of Asherah crumbled.

Elijah felt the hand of God upon him. With newfound energy he ran down the slippery mountainside with not a single false step. As he ran toward Jezreel he heard the voices of the people raised in joy. The Lord God had brought the drought to an end. Tucking up the long ends of his cloak so that he might run faster, Elijah gave a passing nod to King Ahab as he ran past his chariot. The prophet reached the gates of the city before the king.

The news of Elijah's victory over the prophets of Baal on Mount Carmel spread rapidly through the palace. "The Lord God of Israel sent fire and rain, Baal was silent," the people told each other. Elijah had just begun to savor his triumph when he saw a messenger from the queen flanked by members of her personal guard. Suddenly the prophet's legs lost their power. Very slowly he made his way between two of the queen's attendants through the long corridors of the palace.

The queen's back was to the prophet. She was looking out the window, down at the courtyard far

below. Even without seeing her face, Elijah felt a shiver run up his spine. Facing down eight hundred and fifty prophets was easier than one angry queen. Elijah cleared his throat. "You have not called me here to praise my Lord God of Israel's triumph on Carmel this day," he said.

Jezebel turned around and advanced toward Elijah. Her face, pale with rage, was framed with a cloud of pitch-black hair.

Elijah drew back a few steps. "You will do more than tremble before this day is out," she said coldly. Her arms folded across her chest, the queen stared down at Elijah, her mouth twisted in contempt. "You don't seem so high and mighty now, you miserable toad."

"I did only what the Lord God of Israel commanded me," Elijah said. He was afraid to meet the queen's eye. "As your own prophets would follow Baal." As soon as the words were out of his mouth, he knew he had made a mistake.

The queen's hand closed around the amulet at her throat. "By my God, Baal, I swear that by tomorrow I shall make your life what you made of their lives today."

Elijah turned and ran from the chamber, through the palace, across the courtyard, down to the gates of the city. Without pausing for breath, he kept running until he reached Beersheba at the southernmost end of the neighboring kingdom of Judah. "Just when I thought I had won, and the word of the Lord God had triumphed!" Elijah drank thirstily from a brook and bathed his tired feet.

"I'd better keep moving. Queen Jezebel is not a woman of idle threats. As much as I love the Lord God, so she is loyal to her Baal and Asherah."

Alone, hungry, and frightened that the queen's soldiers would follow him even into Judahite territory, Elijah wandered into the desert. He had no food and could find no source of water. Finally he collapsed under a straggly bush and cried aloud to God. "Oh, come and take me now. My life is over. The queen will pursue me until she carries out her threat. Oh, poor Elijah," he wailed. Exhausted, he fell asleep.

Some time later he felt something brush his shoulder. He opened his eyes and saw a round, flat piece of bread, the kind he liked, baked over hot stones. It was still warm. A jar of cool water stood next to it. Suddenly a voice addressed him, although he saw no one nearby.

"Eat and drink," said the divine messenger. Eagerly Elijah seized the food and drank his fill. Then he fell asleep again.

Once again Elijah was startled awake. The messenger placed more bread and water near him. "Get up and eat. Prepare yourself, Elijah. You have a long journey ahead."

"Not again," Elijah muttered to himself. "There is no rest for the prophet of God." Wearily he ate more bread and finished the entire pitcher of water. He journeyed through the barren desert for forty days and forty nights and was not hungry or thirsty again.

Finally Elijah saw Mount Sinai just a few hours ahead of him. His heart pounding, he found the cave

where Moses had been allowed to see the Lord God of Israel. "Now it is my turn," Elijah thought. "I have been brought to the exact place where the Lord God came to Moses in fire and smoke and earthquake." He settled himself in the darkness of the cave to wait for God.

Before long the voice of God sounded through the cave. But it did not thunder. "What are you doing here, Elijah?"

"I have been so loyal, so true to you. For the rest of Israel broke your covenant, destroyed your altars, and silenced your prophets. Remember, I did away with the altars of Baal and his prophets. Only I am left, loyal and true to the Lord God of Israel. And what has happened? Jezebel has sworn revenge. All the people want to kill me."

"Go and stand outside, upon the mountaintop," came the reply. Elijah edged his way to the craggy ledge of Sinai. Suddenly a fierce wind ripped across the mountain, sharp as an ax blade, splitting rocks and shaking the ground under Elijah's feet. Terrified, he squeezed himself into a cleft between two massive rocks and clung to the cold stone, waiting for the Lord God to appear. But the Lord was not in the wind.

The ground heaved under his feet and tore one of the boulders from the side of the mountain. Dodging falling rocks, Elijah stumbled back to the cave and waited. But the Lord was not in the earthquake.

Around Elijah balls of flame blazed among the rocks, then disappeared. But the Lord was not in the fire.

"Wind, earthquake, and fire, thus the Lord appeared to Moses," Elijah pondered nervously.

Expecting thunder, Elijah heard silence. As the silence spread, thick as a carpet around him, Elijah went out from the cave. He quivered and covered his face with his cloak, for he knew that the Lord was present. Out of the silence a voice addressed him, "What are you doing here, Elijah?"

"The Israelites have broken your covenant, destroyed your altars, and silenced your prophets. And I, only I alone am left, loyal and true to the Lord God of Israel."

But God replied, "You and seven thousand others who have not bowed to Baal or kissed his idols. Go down from here, Elijah, and journey across the desert to Damascus. Even though the people there do not worship me as their God, they have seen my power and they know that you are my prophet. In my name you shall anoint Hazael king over Syria. When you return to Israel, you shall anoint Jehu to be king in Ahab's place, and you shall also anoint Elisha to take your place as my prophet."

Wrapping his cloak around him, Elijah made his way down the mountainside, measuring every step.

After many days' journey across the desert, Elijah came to the farming village where Elisha lived. From a distance Elijah saw Elisha plowing in the fields. Drawing near, the prophet took off his cloak and held it out before him. Without a word or further sign, he draped it over the farmer's shoulder. Elisha

followed Elijah, the prophet of God, out of the grain fields to proclaim the word of God.

Some time later Elijah and Elisha were preparing to leave the town of Gilgal.

"You stay here," the old prophet said. "For God has called me to Bethel."

Elisha continued to match his stride to Elijah's. "I shall not leave your side," he protested.

When they reached Bethel, a group of prophets came to meet them. One of them took Elisha aside. "Do you know that this very day the Lord God shall take Elijah, your companion, from your side?"

Elisha answered calmly. "Of course I know. Say nothing."

"You might as well stay here, Elisha," Elijah called. "For God is calling me on to Jericho."

"Then I shall go to Jericho also," the younger man answered. And they headed up the road that wound through the wadi to the east.

They had not yet reached the city gates when a throng of prophets came to greet them. One said to Elisha, "Do you know that today God will take the man who walks by your side?"

"I know all too well," Elisha answered.

Elijah rested his hand on his friend's shoulder. "Stay here with these men. For the Lord calls me on to the banks of the Jordan River."

"Then I shall journey to the Jordan."

Fifty of the prophets followed a short distance behind the two men. When they reached the banks of

the Jordan, Elijah stood at the edge of the water, Elisha by his side. The other men waited a short distance away.

Elijah took his cloak and rolled it up tightly. Stretching out his arm, he struck the water. In an instant the water of the river was parted until there was a path of dry land where a moment earlier there had been only water.

When they had reached the other side of the Jordan, Elijah spoke. "What can I do for you, my friend, before I go?"

Elisha responded without hesitation, "If only I could inherit some of your spirit, to serve the Lord God —"

"You have asked a difficult thing. If you see me as I am being taken from you, then you shall have your wish. But if you do not see me depart, then my power shall not rest upon you."

They walked and talked quietly, knowing that the time was drawing near. Suddenly a chariot of fire pulled by horses with flowing manes of flame separated the two men. Elisha fell back as Elijah was taken up to heaven in the divine whirlwind.

Elisha watched the flaming chariot mounting through the sky. "I have seen the chariot of the Lord God of Israel, the chariot and its horses have passed in front of me," he cried out. Then the chariot carrying Elijah disappeared.

As a sign of mourning for his departed friend, Elisha tore his garments. He then knelt and picked up Elijah's cloak from the ground. Returning alone, he stood on the bank of the Jordan. With the cloak

of Elijah he struck the water and said, "Where is the Lord God of Israel, the God of Elijah?"

As he spoke the waves rolled up, to the one side and to the other. Slowly Elisha walked across a path of dry land and headed for the place across the Jordan where the prophets awaited him.

"The spirit of Elijah rests upon him," they repeated to one another, filled with awe.

Notes

The stories about Elijah the prophet appear in 1 Kings 17, 18, 19, 21, and 2 Kings 1 and 2. Elijah prophesied during the first half of the ninth century B.C.E., during the reign of King Ahab, son of Omri, in the Northern Kingdom of Israel. (The united monarchy of David and Solomon had been split into two kingdoms, Israel in the North and Judah in the South, after the death of Solomon.) Ahab was married to a Phoenician princess, Jezebel, a loyal follower of the god Baal Melqart, who sought to spread her religion to her new subjects. Baal was the Canaanite storm god, and Asherah was an important Canaanite goddess. The Bible uses these names, in the singular or plural, as general designations for the Canaanite deities.

Elijah appears abruptly on the scene as the champion of the Lord God of Israel. The issue at stake is which god, the Lord God of Israel or Baal the storm god, controls the rain, and thus the fertility of the land. Elijah claims that the Lord God of Israel controls the rain and is responsible for the drought. After the contest on Mount Carmel reveals Israel's God as the true God, the Lord God sends rain.

The scene portraying Elijah on Mount Sinai (the biblical text uses the northern name Horeb for the mountain rather than the more familiar southern name, Sinai) forms an ironic contrast to his victory on Mount Carmel. The prophet who stood alone against four hundred prophets of Baal on Mount Carmel is afraid of Queen Jezebel and flees for his life. He goes to Sinai, where God appeared to Moses amid smoke, thunder, and lightning. He journeys forty days to reach the mountain, a reminder of the forty days and forty nights Moses spent on Mount Sinai. The biblical text hints, and we have made it explicit, that Elijah is seeking a revelation of God similar to God's revelation to Moses. God does not appear to Elijah in such a dramatic way, however; Elijah recognizes the presence of God not in visual displays of power but rather in the silence. Moreover, he is reminded that he is not, as he complains, the only remaining faithful follower of the Lord God; there are many others. Elijah's parting of the Jordan River so that he and Elisha can cross over recalls Moses' parting of the sea in the exodus story.

Bibliography

Alter, Robert. *The Art of Biblical Narrative*. Basic Books, 1981.

Amit, Yairah. "Judges 4: Its Contents and Form," pp. 89–111 in *Journal for the Study of the Old Testament* 39, 1987.

Buber, Martin. *Moses*. Harper Torchbooks, 1958.

————. *On the Bible: Eighteen Studies*. Schocken, 1968.

Cansdale, George S. *All the Animals of the Bible Lands*. Zondervan, 1970.

Childs, Brevard S. *The Book of Exodus: A Critical, Theological Commentary*. Westminster, 1974.

Clines, David J. A. *The Theme of the Pentateuch*. JSOT Press, 1982.

Exum, J. Cheryl, " 'A Mother in Israel': A Familiar Figure Reconsidered," pp. 73–85 in *Feminist Interpretation of the Bible*. Westminster, 1985.

————. "Aspects of Symmetry and Balance in the Samson Saga," pp. 3–29 in *Journal for the Study of the Old Testament* 19, 1981.

————. " 'You Shall Let Every Daughter Live': A Study of Exodus 1:8–2:10," pp. 63–82 in *Semeia* 28. Scholars Press, 1983.

Good, Edwin M. *Irony in the Old Testament*. Almond Press, 1981.

Gottwald, Norman K. *The Hebrew Bible: A Socio-Literary Introduction*. Fortress Press, 1985.

Greenstein, Edward L. "The Riddle of Samson," pp. 237–260 in *Prooftexts* 1. Johns Hopkins University Press, 1981.

Gunkel, Hermann. *The Legends of Genesis.* Schocken, 1964 (paperback).

Harper's Bible Atlas. Harper & Row, 1987.

Harper's Bible Commentary. Harper & Row, 1988.

Harper's Bible Dictionary. Harper & Row, 1985.

The Interpreter's Dictionary of the Bible. Abingdon, 4 vols. 1962; supplementary vol. 1976.

Jobling, David. "Myth and Its Limits in Genesis 2.4b–3.24," in *The Sense of Biblical Narrative*, Vol. 2. JSOT Press, 1986.

King, Philip J. *Amos, Hosea, Micah—An Archaeological Commentary.* Westminster, 1988.

McCarter, P. Kyle, Jr. *I Samuel.* Anchor Bible, Vol. 8. Doubleday, 1980.

———. *II Samuel.* Anchor Bible, Vol. 9. Doubleday, 1984.

Meyers, Carol. *Discovering Eve: Ancient Israelite Women in Context.* Oxford University Press, 1988.

Miller, J. Maxwell and Hayes, John H. *A History of Ancient Israel and Judah.* Westminster Press, 1986.

Oxford Bible Atlas. 3rd ed. Oxford University Press, 1984.

Pritchard, J. B. *The Ancient Near East in Pictures.* Princeton University Press, 1954.

Rendtorff, Rolf. *The Old Testament: An Introduction.* Fortress Press, 1985.

Soggin, J. Alberto. *Judges.* Westminster, 1981.

van der Woude, A. S., ed. *The World of the Bible.* Bible Handbook, Vol. 1. Eerdmans, 1986.

de Vaux, Roland. *Ancient Israel: Its Life and Institutions.* McGraw-Hill, 1961.

Wiesel, Elie. *Messengers of God: Biblical Portraits and Legends.* Random House, 1976.

Zohary, Michael. *Plants of the Bible.* Cambridge University Press, 1982.

About the Authors

Alice Bach is the author of more than twenty books for children and young adults, including a series of picture books that has been translated into five languages. Two of her novels have been ALA Notable Books and two have been awarded Best Book of the Year by *The New York Times*. A native New Yorker, she is currently working toward a doctorate in Biblical Studies at Union Theological Seminary.

J. Cheryl Exum is Associate Professor of Hebrew Bible at Boston College. She is well known for her work on the biblical book of Judges and has published widely in the area of literary criticism of biblical texts. She has served on the editorial boards of scholarly journals and is the editor of three volumes on biblical poetics.

The authors wrote part of *Moses' Ark* on a remote Greek island, pretending their hot and dusty hillside was Mount Carmel. They are writing a companion volume, *Miriam's Well*, in the wildernesses of Boston and New York.

About the Illustrators

Leo and Diane Dillon have collaborated on many beautiful and memorable picture books. They were awarded the Caldecott Medal in 1976 and again in 1977, and have received honors from the Society of Illustrators, the Art Directors Club, and the American Institute of Graphic Arts. They graduated from Parsons School of Design and taught at the School of Visual Arts for many years. They live in Brooklyn with their son, Lee, who is an artist.

In working on *Moses' Ark,* the Dillons said, "Our concerns were to be as faithful as possible to the tools, artifacts, clothing, and time of the stories. We concentrated on the feelings in the stories and on the emotions of the people and their involvement in the events, rather than approaching them from a symbolic or sacred point of view. Our inspiration was based on Assyrian and Egyptian reliefs but modernized through our own style."

About the Book

Moses' Ark was designed by Jane Byers Bierhorst. The text is set in Cochin, and the display type is Delphian Roman. It was printed at Orange Graphics in Orange, Virginia.

The illustrations were done in a combination of pastel and watercolor.